Introductory Paper 2

INFORMATION FOR MANAGEMENT CONTROL

For exams in 2007

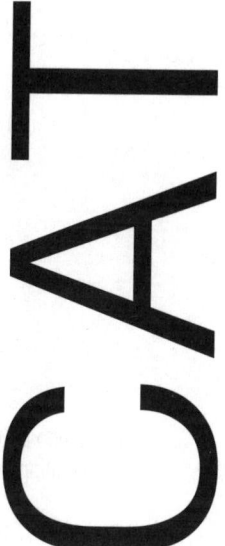
CAT

Practice & Revision Kit

In this January 2007 new edition

- **Do you know?** Checklists to test your knowledge and understanding of topics

- A question and answer bank

- The ACCA's pilot paper as a mock exam

BPP's **i-Pass** product also supports this paper.

BPP
LEARNING MEDIA

First edition 2004
Fourth edition January 2007

ISBN 9780 7517 3555 0 (previous ISBN 0 7517 2571 4)

British Library Cataloguing-in-Publication Data
A catalogue record for this book
is available from the British Library

Published by

BPP Learning Media Ltd
BPP House, Aldine Place
London W12 8AA

www.bpp.com/learningmedia

Printed in Great Britain by
WMP
Frederick Street
Walsall, WS2 9ST

We are grateful to the Association of Chartered
Certified Accountants for permission to reproduce the
pilot paper. The answers to the pilot paper have been
prepared by BPP Learning Media Ltd.

Your learning materials, published by BPP Learning
Media Ltd, are printed on paper sourced from
sustainable, managed forests.

Contents

	Page
Question index	4
Using your BPP Practice and Revision Kit	5
Important information for students taking this exam in 2007	9

Passing CAT exams

How to revise	13
How NOT to revise	14
How to PASS your exam	15
How NOT to PASS your exam	16
Syllabus	17
Approach to examining the syllabus	22
The Computer Based Examination	23
Tackling Multiple Choice Questions	24
Using your BPP products	25
Current issues	26

Questions and answers

Questions	35
Answers	107

Exam practice

Mock exam 1
• Questions	127
• Answers	141

Mock exam 2
• Questions	145
• Answers	159

Review form & free prize draw

Question index

		Marks	Time allocation Mins	Page number Question	Page number Answer

Part A: Computer systems

Computer hardware and software Objective test questions	1–38	76	91	35	107
Computer skills Objective test questions	39–80	84	100	43	109
Security, back-ups and legal issues Objective test questions	81–100	40	48	57	111

Part B: Management information

Introduction to management information and reporting management information Objective test questions	101-120	40	48	63	112
Business organisation and accounting Objective test questions	121-130	20	24	69	113
Management responsibility and performance measurement; cost units, cost classification and profit reporting Objective test questions	131-169	78	93	73	114
Materials, labour costs and overhead costs Objective test questions	170-214	90	108	83	117
Information for comparison, variances, marginal costing and decision making Objective test questions	215-247	66	79	95	121
Mock exam 1 Pilot paper	248-297	100	120	127	141
Mock exam 2	298-347	100	120	145	159

BPP
LEARNING MEDIA

Using your BPP Practice and Revision Kit

Aim of this Practice & Revision Kit

To provide the practice to help you succeed in the computer based examination for Paper 2 *Information for Management Control*.

To pass the examination you need a thorough understanding in all areas covered by the syllabus and teaching guide.

Recommended approach

- Make sure you are able to answer questions on **everything** specified by the syllabus and teaching guide. You cannot make any assumptions about what questions may come up on your paper. The examiners aim to discourage 'question spotting'. In a paper that has objective test questions or a number of shorter questions, the examiner has the opportunity to test a wide area of the syllabus. And an area that has been tested in one sitting can still be tested again in the next sitting.

- Learning is an **active** process. Use the **DO YOU KNOW?** Checklists to test your knowledge and understanding of the topics covered in Paper 2 *Information for Management Control* by filling in the blank spaces. Then check your answers against the **DID YOU KNOW?** Checklists. Do not attempt any questions if you are unable to fill in any of the blanks - go back to your **BPP Interactive Text** and revise first.

- When you are revising a topic, think about the mistakes that you know that you should avoid by writing down **POSSIBLE PITFALLS** at the end of each **DO YOU KNOW?** Checklist.

- Once you have completed the checklists successfully, you should attempt the questions on that topic. Each section has a selection of **OBJECTIVE TEST QUESTIONS**.

- In the exam, each question is worth 2 marks. There are 50 questions in the exam giving a possible total of 100 marks. That gives you 2.4 minutes per question. The pass mark is 50.

- Once you have completed all of the questions in the body of this Practice & Revision Kit, you should attempt the **MOCK EXAM** under examination conditions. This is the ACCA's pilot paper. Check your answers against our answers to find out how well you did.

> **Please see the next page for important information concerning the December 2007 exam.**

Important information

BPP
LEARNING MEDIA

Important information for students sitting this exam in 2007

From the **December 2007** exam, ACCA is internationalising the syllabus for this paper. What this means is the use of international terms – such as inventory rather than stock. Amounts will be shown in $ rather than £.

On the following pages we list the International and UK terms. Where terms such as stock, debtors and creditors appear in this kit, we have added the International term in brackets, eg stock (inventory).

Students sitting the exam in **June** will be examined using UK terms. However, your subsequent CAT papers, apart from UK stream financial reporting and tax papers, will use International terms.

International Accounting Terminology

Below is a short list of the most important terms you are likely to use or come across, together with their international equivalents.

UK term	International term
Profit and loss account	Income statement
Profit and loss reserve (in balance sheet)	Retained earnings
Turnover	Revenue
Debtor account	Account receivable
Debtors (eg 'debtors have increased')	Receivables
Debtor	Customer
Creditor account	Account payable
Creditors (eg 'creditors have increased')	Payables
Creditor	Supplier
Debtors control account	Receivables control account
Creditors control account	Payables control account
Stock	Inventory
Fixed asset	Non-current asset (generally). Tangible fixed assets are usually referred to as 'property, plant and equipment'.
Long-term liability	Non-current liability
Provision (eg for depreciation)	Allowance (You will sometimes see 'provision' used too.)
General ledger	Nominal ledger
VAT	Sales tax
Debentures	Loan notes
£	$

Passing CAT exams

How to revise

☑ Plan your revision

At the start of your revision period, you should draw up a **timetable** to plan how long you will spend on each subject and how you will revise each area. You need to consider the total time you have available and also the time that will be required to revise for other exams you're taking.

☑ Practise Practise Practise

The **more questions** you do, the **more likely you are to pass** the exam. Practising questions will mean that you'll get used to the time pressure of the exam. When the time is up, you should note where you've got to and see how many questions you have completed.

☑ Revise enough

Make sure that your revision covers the breadth of the syllabus, as any topic an come up. However it is true that some topics are **key** – they are an important part of the syllabus or are a particular interest of the examiner – and you need to spend sufficient time revising these.

☑ Deal with your difficulties

Difficult areas are topics you find dull and pointless, or subjects that you found problematic when you were studying them. You mustn't become negative about these topics; instead you should build up your knowledge by reading the **Passcards** and using the **Quick quiz** questions in the Study Text to test yourself. When practising questions in the Kit, go back to the Text if you're struggling.

☑ Learn from your mistakes

Having completed a question you must try to look at your answer critically. As you go through the Kit, it's worth noting any traps you've fallen into, and referring to these notes in the days before the exam. Aim to learn at least one new point from each question you attempt.

☑ Complete the mock exam

You should attempt the **Mock exam** at the end of the Kit under **strict exam conditions**, to gain experience of managing your time and producing answers.

How NOT to revise

☒ Revise selectively

Examiners are well aware that some students try to forecast the contents of exams, and only revise those areas that they think will be examined. In CBA, questions come up in a random fashion and you cannot predict what will come up.

☒ Spend all the revision period reading

You cannot pass the exam just by learning the contents of Passcards, Course Notes or Study Texts. You have to develop your **application skills** by practising questions.

☒ Audit the answers

This means reading the answers and guidance without having attempted the questions. Auditing the answers gives you **false reassurance** that you would have tackled the questions in the best way and made the points that our answers do. The feedback we give in our answers will mean more to you if you've attempted the questions and thought through the issues.

☒ Get bogged down

Don't spend a lot of time worrying about all the minute detail of certain topic areas, and leave yourself insufficient time to cover the rest of the syllabus. Remember that a key skill in the exam is the ability to **concentrate on what's important** and this applies to your revision as well.

☒ Overdo studying

Studying for too long without interruption will mean your studying becomes less effective. A five minute break each hour will help. You should also make sure that you are leading a **healthy lifestyle** (proper meals, good sleep and some times when you're not studying).

How to PASS your exam

☑ Prepare for the day

Make sure you set at least one alarm (or get an alarm call), and allow plenty of time to get to the exam hall. You should have your route planned in advance and should listen on the radio for potential travel problems. You should check the night before to see that you have pens, pencils, erasers, watch, calculator with spare batteries, also exam documentation and evidence of identity.

☑ Plan your time

You need to make sure that you will be answering the correct number of questions, and that you spend the right length of time on each question – this will be determined by the number of marks available. Papers 1–5 are 2 hour papers, so each mark carries a time allocation of 1.2 minutes. This means that a 10-mark question should be completed in 12 minutes, and a 2-mark question in 2.4 minutes.

☑ Read the questions carefully

To score well, you must follow the requirements of the question, understanding what aspects of the subject area are being covered, and the tasks you will have to carry out.

☑ Stay until the end of the exam

Use any spare time to **check and recheck** your script. This includes checking you have filled out the candidate details correctly, you have labelled question parts and workings clearly, you have used headers and underlining effectively and spelling, grammar and arithmetic are correct.

How NOT to Pass your exam

☒ Don't do enough questions

If you don't attempt sufficient questions on the paper, you are making it harder for yourself to pass the exam on the questions that you do attempt. Failing to attempt all of the paper is symptomatic of poor time management.

☒ Rush through the questions without thinking about them properly

If you don't understand a question, read it again before you start guessing.

☒ Get bogged down

Each question is only worth 2 marks. If you really can't do it, move on.

☒ Present your work poorly

Markers will only be able to give you credit if they can read your writing. There are also plenty of other things that will make it more difficult for markers to reward you. Examples include:

- Not using black or blue ink
- Not showing clearly which question you're attempting

Syllabus

Introduction

This booklet contains the Study Guide for the ACCA's Certified Accounting Technician Paper 2: Information for Management Control.

The Study Guide is designed to help you plan your studies and to provide more detailed interpretation of the syllabus for ACCA's Certified Accounting Technician examinations. It contains both the Syllabus and the Study Sessions for the paper, which you can follow when preparing for the examination.

The Syllabus outlines the content of the paper and how that content is examined. The Study Sessions take the syllabus and expand it into teaching or study sessions of similar length. These sessions indicate what the examiner expects of candidates for each part of the syllabus, and therefore gives you guidance in the skills you are expected to demonstrate in the examinations. The time to complete each session will vary according to your individual capabilities and the time you have available to study. Tuition providers offering face-to-face tuition are recommended to design courses with a minimum of two hours tuition per study session. However, repeated coverage of the material is vital to ensure your understanding and recall of the subject. Be sure to practice past examination questions to consolidate your knowledge and read your *student accountant* magazine regularly.

If you have any queries concerning the study guide, please direct them to:

Education Department
ACCA 29 Lincoln's Inn Fields London WC2A 3EE United Kingdom
tel: +44 (0)20 7059 5833 fax: +44 (0)20 7059 5968
e-mail: info@accaglobal.com

Additional information can be accessed on the ACCA website at:
www.accaglobal.com

© The Association of Chartered Certified Accountants
August 2006

ABOUT ACCA
ACCA is the largest and fastest-growing international accountancy body, with over 345,000 students and members in 170 countries. ACCA's reputation is grounded in 100 years of providing quality accounting and financial qualifications. With a predominantly young and dynamic membership, ACCA aims to create value for the profession and the business community.

Information for Management Control

AIMS

To develop the ability to use a computer system safely and effectively and to understand the need for data and information to be kept confidential and secure. To develop knowledge and an understanding of how organisations provide basic management information for decision-making, planning and control.

OBJECTIVES

On completion of this paper, candidates should be able to:

- carry out simple visual safety checks on hardware and follow appropriate powering up and shutting down procedures
- understand the purpose of passwords
- access, amend, save and print documents and other files and exit from the relevant software
- use appropriate computer file and folder names
- follow procedures for taking back-up copies of computer files
- understand different types of risk including viruses and hacking
- understand relevant security and legal regulations covering data protection, copyright, health and safety and record retention
- seek assistance when difficulties occur when working with computers
- recognise the need for management information
- identify different elements of cost
- identify different sources of income and expenditure
- code and extract income and expenditure correctly
- deal with problems / errors correctly
- provide comparisons on costs and income
- use relevant software applications to access, analyse, present and communicate information (accounting package, spreadsheet, word processing, e-mail)
- handle confidential information in the correct manner
- present information using house style.

POSITION OF THE PAPER IN THE OVERALL SYLLABUS

No prior knowledge is required before commencing study for Paper 2. This paper provides the basic techniques required to use a computer system safely and to effectively recognise, provide and maintain management information.

Candidates require a sound understanding of the methods and techniques covered in this paper to enable them to move on to the more complex systems and management control problems covered at subsequent levels.

Some of the methods introduced in this paper are revisited and extended in Paper 4, *Accounting for Costs*.

SYLLABUS CONTENT

1 **Use computer systems safely and effectively**
   (a) Visual safety checks
       (i) hardware components
       (ii) plugs and cables
   (b) Types of system
       (i) stand-alone PC
       (ii) networked system
       (iii) mainframe with terminals

2 **Security, confidentiality and legal issues**
   (a) Confidentiality
       (i) system access controls
       (ii) individual file (document or spreadsheet) protection
   (b) Security
       (i) back-up copies
       (ii) archiving
       (iii) secure storage
       (iv) theft and fraud
   (c) Legal regulations
       (i) data protection legislation
       (ii) VDU regulations
       (iii) computer-related Health and Safety
       (iv) document and record retention

3 **Management information**
   (a) Introduction to management information
       (i) the relationship between financial and management accounting
       (ii) the purpose of management information: decision making, planning and control
   (b) Reporting management information
       (i) methods of extracting, analysing, presenting and communicating information (including letter, memo, report and e-mail message)

Information for Management Control

(ii)   handling confidential information

(iii)   using software to perform (b)(i) and (ii) when relevant

(iv)   understanding of the organisation's accounting systems and administrative procedures

4   Income and expenditure

(a)   Elements of cost

(i)   materials

(ii)   labour (including makeup of gross pay)

(iii)   expenses

(b)   Responsibility centres

(i)   cost centres

(ii)   profit centres

(iii)   investment centres

(c)   Relevant documents / sources of information

(i)   purchase orders and purchase invoices

(ii)   sales orders and sales invoices

(iii)   policy manual

(iv)   payroll

(v)   management reports and spreadsheets

(d)   Organisational structures

(i)   coding systems

(ii)   cost classification

5   Comparisons

(a)   Sources of information for comparison

(i)   previous period data

(ii)   corresponding period data

(iii)   forecast data

(iv)   ledgers

(b)   Variances

(i)   adverse / favourable

(ii)   exception reporting

(iii)   controllable / non-controllable

(iv)   reports

6   Decision-making

(a)   Marginal costing

(i)   contribution

(ii)   break-even

(iii)   margin of safety

(b)   Management information

(i)   extraction from relevant sources

(ii)   use in decision-making

(iii)   role in organisation

EXCLUDED TOPICS

The following topics are specifically excluded from Paper 2:

- software and systems development
- database design and database software.

KEY AREAS OF THE SYLLABUS

All areas of the syllabus are equally important.

APPROACH TO EXAMINING THE SYLLABUS

The examination is a two-hour paper. It can be taken as a written paper or as a computer based exam. Assessment will be based on multiple choice questions covering the breadth of the syllabus, testing that candidates have acquired the necessary knowledge of the areas identified above.

	No. of marks
50 multiple choice questions:	100

Information for Management Control

STUDY SESSIONS

1 Nature, safety and use of computer systems

(a) Describe the different types of hardware configuration: stand-alone PC, networked system, mainframe with terminals

(b) Explain where the different types of hardware configuration may be used

(c) Describe the hardware and software components of a computer system

(d) Describe simple visual safety checks on computer hardware and ancillaries (plugs and cables) and explain their importance

(e) Describe the correct process for powering up and for shutting down computer systems

(f) Describe how to save, transfer and print documents

(g) Outline the requirements of health and safety legislation related to the use of computer hardware

2 Computer system confidentiality and security

(a) Explain computer system access controls and procedures for individual file protection

(b) Describe procedures for backing-up, archiving and storing information securely

(c) Discuss the prevention of computer fraud and data corruption, and of hardware/software problems and failure

(d) Discuss security issues related to the location of hardware and software

(e) Outline the requirements of data protection legislation relating to computer software/information

3 Introduction to management information

(a) Discuss the purpose of management information: planning, control and decision-making

(b) Distinguish between data and information

(c) Describe the features of useful management information

(d) Describe and identify sources and categories of information

(e) Compare cost and management accounting with external financial reporting

(f) Explain the limitations of cost and management accounting information

(g) Describe the accounting technician's role in a cost and management accounting system

4 Reporting management information

(a) Discuss methods of analysing, presenting and communicating information

(b) Describe the nature of general purpose application software packages, including word processing and spreadsheets

(c) Identify suitable formats for communicating management information according to purpose

(d) Identify the general principles of distributing reports (e.g. procedures, timing, recipients) including the reporting of confidential information

(e) Interpret information presented in management reports

5 Aspects of business organisation and accounting

(a) Describe the organisation, and main functions, of an office as a centre for information and administration

(b) Describe the function and use of a manual of policies, procedures and best practices

(c) Identify the main types of transactions undertaken by a business and the key personnel involved in initiating, processing and completing transactions

(d) Discuss the need for effective control over transactions

(e) Explain and illustrate the principles and practice of double-entry book-keeping

(f) Describe and illustrate the use of ledgers and prime entry records in both integrated and interlocking accounting systems

(g) Identify the key features, functions and benefits of a computerised accounting system

6 Management responsibility and performance measurement

(a) Explain and illustrate the concept of cost centres

(b) Explain and illustrate the concept of profit centres

(c) Explain and illustrate the concept of investment centres

(d) Describe performance measures appropriate to cost, profit and investment centres (cost / profit per unit / % of sales; efficiency, capacity utilisation and production volume ratios; ROCE / RI, asset turnover)

(e) Apply performance measures appropriate to cost, profit and investment centres

Information for Management Control

7 Cost units, cost classification and profit reporting

(a) Explain and illustrate the concept of cost units

(b) Describe the variety of cost classifications used for different purposes in a cost accounting system, including by responsibility, function, behaviour, direct/indirect

(c) Describe and illustrate the nature of variable, fixed and mixed (semi-variable, stepped-fixed) costs

(d) Describe and illustrate the classification of material and labour costs

(e) Prepare, and explain the nature and purpose of, profit statements in absorption and marginal costing formats

(f) Calculate the cost of a product or service

8 Elements of cost

(a) Describe and illustrate the accounting for material costs (NB stock issue pricing is excluded)

(b) Calculate material requirements, making allowance for sales and product/material stock changes (NB control levels and EOQ are excluded)

(c) Describe and illustrate the accounting for labour costs (including overtime premiums and idle time)

(d) Prepare an analysis of gross earnings

(e) Explain and illustrate labour remuneration methods

(f) Calculate the effect of remuneration methods and changes in productivity on unit labour costs

(g) Explain and illustrate the process of cost apportionment and absorption for indirect costs (excluding reciprocal services)

9 Source documents and coding

(a) Explain the use of codes in categorising and processing transactions and the importance of correct coding

(b) Describe the material control cycle (including the concept of 'free' stock, but excluding control levels and EOQ) and the documentation necessary to order, receive, store and issue materials

(c) Describe the procedures required to ensure the correct authorisation, coding, analysis and recording of direct and indirect material costs

(d) Describe the procedures and documentation required to ensure the correct coding, analysis and recording of direct and indirect labour costs

(e) Describe the procedures and documentation required to ensure the correct authorisation, coding, analysis and recording of direct and indirect expenses

(f) Describe the procedures and documentation to ensure the correct coding, analysis and recording of sales

10 Information for comparison

(a) Explain the purpose of making comparisons

(b) Identify relevant bases for comparison: previous period data, corresponding period data, forecast/budget data

(c) Explain the forecasting/budgeting process and the concept of feedforward and feedback control

(d) Explain the concept of flexible budgets

(e) Use appropriate income and expenditure data for comparison

11 Variances

(a) Explain the concept of exception reporting

(b) Calculate variances between current actual and historical/forecast data which may or may not be adjusted for volume change (N.B. standard costing is excluded)

(c) Identify whether variances are favourable or adverse

(d) Identify possible causes of variances

(e) Explain factors affecting the decision whether to investigate variances

12 Marginal costing and decision-making

(a) Explain and illustrate the concept of contribution

(b) Calculate and utilise contribution per unit, per £ of sales and per unit of limiting factor

(c) Explain and calculate the break-even point and the margin of safety

(d) Analyse the effect on break-even point and margin of safety of changes in selling price and cost

(e) Describe the assumptions, uses and limitations of marginal costing and break-even analysis

Approach to examining the Syllabus

Paper 2 is a two-hour paper. It can be taken as a written paper or a computer based examination. (See page 23 for information on computer based examinations.)

The examination, whether taken in written form or as a computer based exam, consists of fifty compulsory multiple choice questions. Each question is worth two marks.

Analysis of pilot paper

Pilot paper (written examination)

Fifty multiple choice questions covering various computer systems and management information topics.

This paper is reproduced as Mock exam 1 at the back of this Practice & Revision Kit.

The Computer Based Examination

The ACCA has introduced a computer based examination (CBE) for CAT Papers 1–4 (in addition to the conventional paper based examination).

Computer based examinations must be taken at an ACCA CBE Licensed Centre.

How does CBE work?

- Questions are displayed on a monitor

- Candidates enter their answer directly onto the computer

- Candidates have two hours to complete the examination

- When the candidate has completed their examination, the computer automatically marks the file containing the candidate's answers

- Candidates are provided with a certificate showing their results before leaving the examination room

- The CBE Licensed Centre uploads the results to the ACCA (as proof of the candidate's performance) within 48 hours

Benefits

- **Flexibility** as a CBE can be sat at any time.

- **Resits** can also be taken at any time and there is no restriction on the number of times a candidate can sit a CBE.

- **Instant feedback** as the computer displays the results at the end of the CBE.

- Results are notified to ACCA **within 48 hours**.

- **Extended closing date periods** (see ACCA website for further information)

CBE question types

- Multiple choice – choose one answer from four options

CAT CBE

You will have two hours in which to answer a number of questions, which are worth a total of 100 marks. See the ACCA website for a demonstration and up to date information (www.acca.org.uk/colleges/cbe_demo).

Tackling Multiple Choice Questions

MCQs feature in both the paper and computer-based papers.

The MCQs in your exam contain four possible answers. You have to **choose the option that best answers the question**. The three incorrect options are called distracters. There is a skill in answering MCQs quickly and correctly. By practising MCQs you can develop this skill, giving you a better chance of passing the exam.

You may wish to follow the approach outlined below, or you may prefer to adapt it.

Step 1   Skim read all the MCQs and identify what appear to be the easier questions.

Step 2   Attempt each question – **starting with the easier questions** identified in Step 1. Read the question **thoroughly**. You may prefer to work out the answer before looking at the options, or you may prefer to look at the options at the beginning. Adopt the method that works best for you.

Step 3   Read the four options and see if one matches your own answer. Be careful with numerical questions as the distracters are designed to match answers that incorporate common errors. Check that your calculation is correct. Have you followed the requirement exactly? Have you included every stage of the calculation?

Step 4   You may find that none of the options matches your answer.

- Re-read the question to ensure that you understand it and are answering the requirement
- Eliminate any obviously wrong answers
- Consider which of the remaining answers is the most likely to be correct and select the option

Step 5   If you are still unsure make a note and continue to the next question

Step 6   Revisit unanswered questions. When you come back to a question after a break you often find you are able to answer it correctly straight away. If you are still unsure have a guess. You are not penalised for incorrect answers, so **never leave a question unanswered!**

After extensive practice and revision of MCQs, you may find that you recognise a question when you sit the exam. Be aware that the detail and/or requirement may be different. If the question seems familiar read the requirement and options carefully – do not assume that it is identical.

Using your BPP products

This Kit gives you the question practice and guidance you need in the exam. Our other products can also help you pass:

- **Learning to Learn Accountancy** gives further valuable advice on revision

- **Passcards** provide you with clear topic summaries and exam tips

- **Success CDs** help you revise on the move

- **i-Pass CDs** offer tests of knowledge against the clock

- **Learn Online** is an e-learning resource delivered via the Internet, offering comprehensive tutor support and featuring areas such as study, practice, email service, revision and useful resources

You can purchase these products by visiting www.bpp.com/mybpp.

Visit our website www.bpp.com/acca/learnonline to sample aspects of Learn Online free of charge.

Current issues

The examiner has recently written two articles in the Student Accountant which are relevant to CAT Paper 2. The article on variances has been reproduced on the next page. Make sure that you read and understand this article. You need to be able to calculate the three cost variances and the three revenue variances and say whether they are favourable or adverse. Note that the article describes the different causes of variances and lists a number of factors which may affect whether or not a variance is investigated. Make sure you know these. Relevant questions in this Practice & Revision Kit are questions 220 to 233 and there are some more examples on pages 30 to 31.

The second article written by the examiner was in the August 2006 edition of Student Accountant and was relevant to CAT Papers 2 and 4. This is worth reading but don't worry too much about the calculations as these are relevant to CAT Paper 4. This can be found on the ACCA website at www.accaglobal.com. Relevant questions in this Practice & Revision Kit are questions 208 to 214.

Examiner's article on variances

calculating variances
relevant to CAT Scheme Paper 2

in comparison

■ Students are introduced to the idea of making comparisons in CAT Paper 2. This could be a comparison between financial information for the current period and corresponding information for a previous period, or between current financial information and corresponding information previously forecast/budgeted for the same period. Such comparisons inevitably result in a variation (or variances) because the two sets of information are different.

CAT Paper 2 students need to be able to:
☐ calculate variances
☐ identify whether variances are favourable or adverse
☐ identify possible causes of variances
☐ explain factors affecting the decision whether or not to investigate variances.

The main focus of this article is on the calculation of variances. In addition, the three other objectives listed above will also be considered. The article, in illustrating the calculation of variances, will be concerned only with the comparison of actual results with budgeted results for a given period. However, exactly the same principles apply to the comparison of actual results for one period with those of another.

CALCULATING VARIANCES
Profit variances, between current performance and forecast/budget or between a current and previous period, may result from variances in revenues and/or costs. Revenue variances occur for one or both of the following main reasons:
☐ a change in the level of activity (quantity sold)
☐ a change in the selling price.

Cost variances occur for one or more of three main reasons:

☐ a change in the level of activity (quantity sold/produced)
☐ a change in the price paid for resources
☐ a change in the efficiency with which resources are used.

Later studies (for CAT Paper 7) will look at the analysis of cost variances in terms of price and efficiency (resulting from the application of standard costing). However, in CAT Paper 2, these two aspects are not separated. As a result, there are two cost variances:
☐ a variance resulting from a change in activity
☐ a variance resulting from changes in price and/or efficiency.

FLEXED BUDGETS
If total variances are going to be divided into activity variances on the one hand, and price/efficiency variances on the other, then the concept of a flexed budget is important. A flexed budget is an adjusted budget (adjusted from the original fixed budget set before a period commences) to reflect what budgeted revenues and costs would have been if set at the actual level of activity. This enables:
☐ activity variances to be calculated through the comparison of the original fixed budget and the flexed budget
☐ price/efficiency variances to be calculated through the comparison of the flexed budget and the actual financial results.

With a flexed revenue budget, it will always be assumed (for CAT Paper 2) that the selling price is a constant and thus a relative (%) change in activity would result in the same % change in total sales revenue.

Key to the preparation of an adjusted (flexed) budget for costs is cost behaviour. For CAT Paper 2, costs are assumed to be either:

☐ absolutely *fixed* in total – the same budgeted expenditure would be incurred regardless of the level of activity
or
☐ proportionately *variable* with activity level – the same relative (%) change in activity would result in the same % change in total budgeted variable costs.

Direct costs (material and labour) will always fall into the category of proportionately variable costs.

REVENUE VARIANCES
The following example illustrates the calculation of revenue variances.

Question
A company sells a single product. The sales budget for a period comprised the sale of 7,000 units at a selling price of £3.40 per unit. 7,260 units were actually sold in the period for a total revenue of £24,321.

What are the revenue variances for the period?

Answer
The fixed sales revenue budget for the period (ie the original budget) is:

7,000 units @ £3.40 per unit = £23,800

The flexed budget calculates the revised sales revenue expected, based on the actual sales volume at the budgeted selling price. Therefore:

7,260 units @ £3.40 per unit = £24,684

The *activity (volume) variance* is £884 (£23,800 - £24,684). The variance is *favourable* because more units were sold than originally budgeted (260 units @ £3.40 per unit). A comparison between the flexed budget and the actual sales revenue yields the *selling price variance*. Therefore:

£24,684 - £24,321 = £363

The variance is *adverse* because the actual sales revenue, from the sale of 7,260 units, is less than the flexed sales budget. The actual selling price achieved of £3.35 per unit (£24,321 ÷ 7,260 units) is £0.05 below the budgeted selling price.

The *total sales revenue variance* (comparing the original budgeted sales revenue with the actual sales revenue) is £521 (£23,800 - £24,321). The variance is *favourable* (more sales revenue than the original budget), and is the sum of the activity (volume) variance and the selling price variance (ie £884 favourable + £363 adverse = £521 favourable).

MULTIPLE-CHOICE QUESTIONS REQUIRING CALCULATION OF SALES VARIANCES

Multiple-choice questions (MCQs) set in CAT Paper 2 exams may require any of the following sales variances to be calculated:
1 the *total* variance between the fixed budget and the actual sales revenue (the total of activity and price changes)

2 the variance due to *activity* change (measuring the difference between the fixed budget and the flexed budget, both based on budgeted selling price)
3 the variance due to *selling price* change (measuring the difference between the flexed budget and the actual sales revenue).

If an MCQ asks for a total sales revenue variance, without any reference to a flexed budget, then the total variance (1) is required. If there is no mention of the original budgeted sales volume, or if the actual sales volume is the same as the budget, then the selling price

technical

variance (3) is all that can be calculated. If complete information, about both budgeted and actual performance is provided, then the specific question requirement will be made clear (eg sales revenue variance comparing actual with the flexed budget).

COST VARIANCES
The following example illustrates the calculation of cost variances.

Question
Budgeted and actual production of Product Z for a period was:

Budget 50,000 units
Actual 51,300 units

The budgeted direct materials cost of the product is £2.80 per unit, and a total of £141,588 was incurred on direct materials in the period.

What are the direct materials variances for the period?

Answer
The fixed budget for the period for direct materials (ie the original budget) is:

50,000 units @ £2.80 per unit = £140,000

The flexed budget calculates the revised direct materials costs expected, based on actual production at the budgeted unit cost. Therefore:

51,300 units @ £2.80 per unit = £143,640

The *activity (volume) variance* is *£3,640* (£140,000 - £143,640). The variance is *adverse* because more units were produced compared with the original budget, incurring additional direct materials costs (1,300 units @ £2.80 per unit). Sales of the additional units will result in a favourable revenue activity variance, which offsets the adverse cost activity variance.

The difference between the flexed budget and the actual costs incurred is the *variance due to changes in the purchase price and/or*

efficiency of usage of the direct materials compared with budget. Therefore:

£143,640 - £141,588 = £2,052

The variance is *favourable* because the direct materials cost incurred in the production of 51,300 units was less than the flexed budget allowance for that level of activity. The actual cost of £2.76 per unit (£141,588 ÷ 51,300 units) is £0.04 per unit lower than the budgeted unit cost.

The *total direct materials cost variance* (comparing the original budgeted direct materials cost with the actual costs incurred) is *£1,588* (£140,000 - £141,588). The variance is *adverse* (more cost incurred than the original budget), and is the sum of the activity (volume) and price/efficiency variances (£3,640 adverse + £2,052 favourable = £1,588 adverse).

MCQs REQUIRING CALCULATION OF COST VARIANCES
MCQs set in CAT Paper 2 exams may require any of the following cost variances to be calculated:
1   the *total* variance between the fixed budget and the actual costs incurred (the total of activity and price/efficiency changes)
2   the variance due to *activity* change (measuring the difference between the fixed budget and the flexed budget, both based on budgeted unit cost)
3   the variance due to *price/efficiency* change (measuring the difference between the flexed budget and the actual costs incurred).

If an MCQ asks for a total cost variance (eg the total direct material cost variance), without any reference to a flexed budget, then the total variance (1) is required. If there is no mention of the original budgeted production volume, or if the actual production volume is the same as the budget, then the price/efficiency variance (3) is all that can be calculated. If complete information, about both budgeted and actual performance is provided then the specific question requirement will be made clear (eg cost variance comparing actual with the flexed budget).

CAUSES AND INVESTIGATION OF VARIANCES
There are a number of possible causes of variances, some that management can control, and others that are less controllable.

In the case of sales activity (volume), it is inevitable that variances occur as it is difficult to accurately predict customer demand, and a change in the economic environment could affect the whole market. This is frequently uncontrollable. Sales volume changes may, however, arise as a consequence of management decisions regarding the marketing mix. Such decisions may affect competitive position and could be said to be more controllable. Sales volume variances obviously have a knock-on effect on production volume.

Selling price variances should be within the control of management, but adverse variances can often be justified. Price variances could arise from tactical/strategic decisions taken by management, or simply from a need to match competitor pricing.

Cost price variances may result from largely uncontrollable market forces, but also from poor negotiation or purchasing, from buying a different quality of resources, or even from an inaccurately set budget.

Cost efficiency variances are more likely to be controllable and may result from factors such as staff training, machine maintenance, employee morale, quality of supervision, economies of scale, or resource quality.

A number of factors may affect the decision as to whether or not to investigate a variance. These include:
☐ the size of the variance
☐ whether the variance is likely to be controllable
☐ whether the likely cause of the variance is already known
☐ whether there is a trend to the variance over a period of time
☐ possible links to other variances
☐ the likely cost of investigation
☐ whether investigation is likely to result in, or affect, any action being taken.

Nigel Coulthurst is examiner for CAT Papers 2 and 4

Now that you have read the article on variances you should know that there are three *revenue* variances and three *cost* variances.

Revenue variances	*Cost variances*

- Total sales revenue
- Activity (quantity) variance
- Selling price variance

- Total direct cost variance
- Activity (quantity) variance
- Purchase price/efficiency of usage variance

Here are some examples of questions you might see in the exam.

Revenue variance – example 1

A company sells a single product M. The sales budget for the period of December is 4,500 units at a selling price of $3.10 per unit. 4,850 units were actually sold in December for a total revenue of $14,550.

What is the total sales revenue variance?

Answer

	$	
Revenue should have been (budget)	13,950	(4,500 units × $3.10)
Revenue actually was	14,550	
Total sales revenue variance	600	(Favourable)

Revenue variance – example 2

A company sells a single type of product H. The selling price budget is $4.40 per unit for the month of June. 7,260 units were sold in June for a total revenue of $24,321. The original budgeted sales volume was 7,500 units.

Calculate the activity variance.

Answer

Budgeted sales volume	7,500	
Actual sales volume	7,260	
Activity variance in units	240	Units (Adverse)
× budgeted selling price per unit	× $4.40	
Activity variance	$1,056	(Adverse)

Revenue variance – example 3

Budgeted and actual sales of product C for a period were:

	Units	Selling price per unit $
Budget	10,000	5,20
Actual	12,500	

Total revenue during the period was $66,250.

What is the sales revenue variance comparing actual with the flexed budget?

> **Helping hand.** The question is asking for the selling price variance.

Answer

	$	
Sales revenue from 12,500 units should have been (× $5.20)	65,000	
But was	66,250	
Selling price variance	1,250	(Favourable)

Cost variance – example 1

A company sells a single type of product X. The budgeted production for a period was 30,000 units at a cost of $3.20 per unit for direct materials. The actual number of units produced was 31,500 and $97,650 was incurred on direct materials in this period.

What is the total direct cost variance?

Answer

	$	
Material should have cost	96,000	(30,000 units × $3.20)
Material did cost	97,650	
	1,650	(Adverse)

Cost variance – example 2

7,260 units of product M were produced in a period at a direct material cost of $29,040. The budgeted direct materials volume was 7,000 units and the budgeted cost was $3.90 per unit.

Calculate the activity variance.

Answer

Budgeted production volume	7,000	
Actual production volume	7,260	
Activity variance in units	260	(Adverse)
× budgeted cost per unit	× $3.90	
Activity variance	$1,014	(Adverse)

Cost variance – example 3

Budgeted and actual production of product K for a period was:

	Units	Direct material cost per unit
Budget	8,000	$4.70
Actual	7,950	

Total direct materials costs for the period were $36,570.

What is the direct material cost variance comparing actual with the flexed budget?

> **Helping hand.** The question is asking for the purchase price variance.

Answer

	$	
7,950 units should have cost (× $4.70)	37,365	
But did cost	36,570	
	795	(Favourable)

Questions

Do you know? – Computer hardware and software

Check that you can fill in the blanks in the statements below before you attempt any questions. If in doubt, you should go back to Chapter 1 of your BPP Interactive Text and revise.

- A computer may be defined as a device which will accept **i**......... data, **p**......... it according to programmed logical and arithmetic rules and store or **o**......... data.

- The **p**.................. is at the heart of any computer. It consists of an arithmetic and logic unit, a control unit and a memory. Important concepts are clock speed (MHz) and RAM.

- Data may be input manually via a keyboard. Alternatively, data may be input using some automated system. The ideal method of data input in a given application is one which minimises input **t**......, **c**...... and **e**.......

- The most common types of storage are magnetic **d**........., magnetic **t**......... and **o**......... **d**......... (eg CD and DVD).

- A **L**...... **A**...... **N**......... is a system of linked PCs and other devices such as printers all located relatively close together. A **W**...... **A**...... **N**......... is a network of computers which are dispersed on a wider geographical scale than LANs.

- **C**.........-**s**......... computing is a configuration in which desktop PCs are regarded as 'clients' that request access to the services available on a more powerful server PC, such as access to a file, e-mail, or printing facilities.

- A **m**......... is needed at either end of a conventional telecommunications link to convert digital signals into analogue signals and vice versa.

- Faster telecommunications networks such as **I**.........**N** and **A**.........**L** have been developed. 'Fast' links to the Internet are sometimes referred to as **b**.............

- **O**............ system software manages computer resources and supervises the running of other programs. It provides a 'bridge' between software programs and the hardware.

- The most widely used operating system is Microsoft **W**............., which is available in a range of versions for both PCs and networks. Other operating systems include Novell Netware, the Mac OS system, Unix and Linux.

- Dialogue design refers to the messages that the computer system displays on screen and the ways that users can respond. Modern systems use **g**............ **u**......... **i**.............

- User friendliness is enhanced by good screen design, intuitiveness, consistency between packages, on-screen **h**........., dialogue boxes, escapability and customisation.

- Software which processes data for a particular purpose, or which is written for a particular data processing function, is known as **a**............ software. An example is a payroll package.

TRY QUESTIONS 1 TO 38

- *Possible pitfalls. Write down examples of mistakes you should avoid.*

  -
  -
  -
  -

Did you know? – Computer hardware and software

Could you fill in the blanks? The answers are in bold. Use this page for revision purposes as you approach the exam.

- A computer may be defined as a device which will accept **input** data, **process** it according to programmed logical and arithmetic rules and store or **output** data.

- The **processor** is at the heart of any computer. It consists of an arithmetic and logic unit, a control unit and a memory. Important concepts are clock speed (MHz) and RAM.

- Data may be input manually via a keyboard. Alternatively, data may be input using some automated system. The ideal method of data input in a given application is one which minimises input **time**, **cost** and **errors**.

- The most common types of storage are magnetic **disk**, magnetic **tape** and **optical disk** (eg CD and DVD).

- A **Local Area Network** is a system of linked PCs and other devices such as printers all located relatively close together. A **Wide Area Network** is a network of computers which are dispersed on a wider geographical scale than LANs.

- **Client-server** computing is a configuration in which desktop PCs are regarded as 'clients' that request access to the services available on a more powerful server PC, such as access to a file, e-mail, or printing facilities.

- A **modem** is needed at either end of a conventional telecommunications link to convert digital signals into analogue signals and vice versa.

- Faster telecommunications networks such as **ISDN** and **ADSL** have been developed. 'Fast' links to the Internet are sometimes referred to as **broadband**.

- **Operating** system software manages computer resources and supervises the running of other programs. It provides a 'bridge' between software programs and the hardware.

- The most widely used operating system is Microsoft **Windows**, which is available in a range of versions for both PCs and networks. Other operating systems include Novell Netware, the Mac OS system, Unix and Linux.

- Dialogue design refers to the messages that the computer system displays on screen and the ways that users can respond. Modern systems use **graphical user interfaces**.

- User friendliness is enhanced by good screen design, intuitiveness, consistency between packages, on-screen **help**, dialogue boxes, escapability and customisation.

- Software which processes data for a particular purpose, or which is written for a particular data processing function, is known as **applications** software. An example is a payroll package.

TRY QUESTIONS 1 TO 38

- *Possible pitfalls include the following (you may have thought of others).*

    - **Not understanding the role of different parts of a computer.**

    - **Being able to describe input, output and storage media but not understanding when their use is appropriate.**

    - **Failing to understand networks including LANs and WANs and the principle of client-server systems.**

    - **Being unable to distinguish between the different types of software.**

Objective test questions 1–38: Computer hardware and software

1   A CD-ROM is an optical storage device. What does CD-ROM stand for?

A   Computer disk read-only memory
B   Control disk read-only memory
C   Compact disk read-only memory
D   Central disk read-only memory

2   Peripherals refer to

A   Printers and scanners
B   External storage devices such as a Zip drive
C   Computer mice
D   All of the above

3   Which **one** of the following companies assembles/produces Personal Computers?

A   Microsoft
B   Dell
C   Google
D   AOL

4   Which **one** of the following is **not** hardware?

A   Printer
B   CPU
C   Microsoft Word
D   Keyboard

5   Which **one** of the following is an input device?

A   Screen
B   Keyboard
C   Printer
D   CPU

6   Input, output and storage devices are often referred to as peripherals. Which **one** of the following is **not** a peripheral?

A   Modem
B   Mouse
C   Scanner
D   Windows XP

7   Computers can be described by type. What type of computer would you usually find on a desk in an office?

A   Mainframe
B   PC
C   Supercomputer
D   Palmtop

8   A PC has three major components. Which **one** of the following is **not** a PC component?

    A   Input devices
    B   CPU
    C   VDU
    D   Printer

9   A computer is made up of three main parts. Which **one** of the following is **not** part of the processor?

    A   Operating system
    B   Control Unit
    C   ALU
    D   Memory

10   Memory is measured in bytes. How many bytes is 16 MB?

    A   1,024
    B   8,388,608
    C   16,777,216
    D   17,179,184

11   Computer data is frequently stored on disk. Which of the following would you expect to have the greatest storage capacity?

    A   CD
    B   Floppy disk
    C   Hard disk
    D   DVD

12   Data can be stored on a variety of mediums. Which **one** of the following is **not** a storage medium?

    A   Mouse
    B   CD-ROM
    C   Magnetic tape
    D   Zip disk

13   Which **one** of the following is **not** a likely advantage of automated input techniques over keyboard input using ten data input clerks?

    A   Speed
    B   Reduced cost
    C   Less administration
    D   Ability to interpret what is being input

14   User-friendly systems can include a number of features. Which **one** of the following is **not** user-friendly.

    A   GUI
    B   WIMP
    C   Icons
    D   Disk operating system (DOS)

15   Documentation reading methods enable the computer to read data direct. Which **one** of the following is **not** a document reading method?

    A   OCR
    B   OMR
    C   WISIWYG
    D   MICR

16   Which of the following is **not** true? A laser printer

    A   Can print graphics
    B   Can print in a variety of different fonts
    C   Can use continuous stationery
    D   May be connected to a laptop computer

17   Which of the following statements is **incorrect**? A Local Area Network (LAN)

    A   Relies on telephone lines to link it together

    B   Consists of a number of independent computers which require network software to function as a network

    C   Is incapable of extensive geographical dispersion

    D   Is likely to contain a central server computer

18   An organisation has recently introduced a scanner and OCR software to 'digitise' information received on paper. Which of the following is **not** a likely benefit of this?

    A   Savings in staff costs
    B   Easier access to information as it is stored in digital form
    C   Quicker input process
    D   Reduced need to take back-ups

19   Which **one** of the following statements, all of which relate to the use of commonly-used input, output and storage devices in a business's computer system, is **correct**?

    A   Dot matrix printers have largely replaced laser printers
    B   The traditional 'wheeled' mouse is gradually being replaced by the optical mouse
    C   Modems often form part of a Local Area Network (LAN)
    D   When shut down, a computer's cache stores the current date.

20   The following statements relate to the electronic point of sale (EPOS) computer technology used by many retail businesses such as supermarkets.

    (i)   EPOS technology makes it possible for shops to calculate customers' bills quickly and accurately.

    (ii)   Shops which use EPOS technology never make mistakes when calculating customers' bills.

    (iii)   EPOS technology enables store groups to hold lower levels of stocks of goods for sale at their retail outlets.

    (iv)   EPOS technology enables a store group to collect data providing information on the shopping patterns of the business's customers.

    Which of the above are **correct**?

    A   (i) and (ii) only
    B   (ii) and (iii) only
    C   (iii) and (iv) only
    D   (i), (iii) and (iv) only

21 Which **one** of the following statements about a desk-top computer's Read Only Memory (ROM) is **false**?

A   ROM is fixed in the computer's hardware
B   ROM cannot be altered in the normal course of processing
C   The application currently being processed is stored in the ROM
D   Information stored in the ROM is used to start up the computer

22 Which **one** of the following statements about a personal computer's Random Access Memory (RAM) is **false**?

A   RAM is an important factor in determining the speed at which a computer 'works'

B   The more RAM there is available, the more processing can be performed without further reference to the hard disk

C   RAM holds data relating to the application currently being processed

D   The amount of RAM cannot ever be changed

23 Which one of the following distinguishes a LAN from a WAN?

A   The number of users on the system
B   The power of the computers in the network
C   The nature of the links between computers
D   The operating system installed on users' computers

24 All the following statements refer to electronic point of sale (EPOS) technology.

(i)   EPOS technology enables a business to assess which items of stock are selling quickly.

(ii)   EPOS technology can be used only by businesses selling durable goods as it is less suited to perishable products.

(iii) EPOS technology can facilitate electronic data interchange links between a retail business and its suppliers.

(iv)   EPOS technology can facilitate the just-in-time (JIT) organisation of production.

Which of the above are **correct**?

A   (i), (ii) and (iv) only
B   (i) and (iv) only
C   (i), (iii) and (iv) only
D   (ii) and (iii) only

25 Which one of the following statements about a desktop computer's random access memory (RAM) is **true**?

A   Information stored in the RAM is used to start up the computer
B   The total amount of RAM built into the computer cannot be increased
C   The application currently being used is stored temporarily in the RAM
D   In the event of a computer crash, information stored in the RAM cannot be lost

26 Which **one** of the following statements about a desk-top computer's read-only memory (ROM) is **true**?

A   The application currently being used is stored temporarily in the ROM

B   In the case of a computer with a CD-ROM drive, all the computer's ROM is externally stored on compact discs

C   In the event of a computer crash, information stored in the ROM is usually lost

D   Information stored in the ROM is used to start up the computer

27   Which **one** of the following is **not** applications software?

   A   Database software
   B   Word-processing software
   C   Software which gives priority to different programs during processing
   D   Software designed in-house to perform a particular task for a particular user

28   Which one of the following statements is **incorrect**? Mainframes differ from PCs because:

   A   Mainframes have larger storage capacity

   B   Data held on a mainframe can be backed-up to tape. Data held on a PC can only be backed up to disks

   C   Mainframes are physically larger

   D   Many mainframes use Unix operating systems whereas with PCs the Windows operating system dominates

29   A smart card is:

   A   A plastic card with machine-sensible data recorded on a magnetic stripe
   B   A plastic card with machine-sensible data recorded on a microchip
   C   A credit card with a security hologram
   D   A hand-held device used to scan text

30   The system operated at many businesses whereby a customer's bank account is debited with the price of goods purchased at the time of the sale is known as:

   A   EFTPOS
   B   POS
   C   EPOS
   D   EFT

31   'Modem' is derived from two words. They are:

   A   Modern demographics
   B   Modulate demodulate
   C   Modular demonstration
   D   Model manager

32   A computer is advertised as having a 750 MHz processor. What processor speed does this indicate?

   A   750 million cycles, or separate instructions, per millisecond
   B   750 million cycles, or separate instructions, per second
   C   750 million cycles, or separate instructions, per minute
   D   750 million cycles, or separate instructions, per hour

33   Which of the following is a device for converting digital signals to analogue signals and then back again?

   A   Transformer
   B   Modem
   C   Packet Switcher
   D   Interpreter

34   The clock speed of a computer is usually measured in Megahertz (MHz). Which of the following does 1 MHz refer to?

    A   1 thousand cycles per second
    B   1 million cycles per second
    C   1 million cycles per minute
    D   1 thousand cycles per minute

35   Many computers have a small, but fast, area of memory that stores a second copy of the data most recently read or written to the main memory.

    A   Cache Memory
    B   Random Access Memory
    C   Read Only Memory
    D   Solid State Memory

36   ISDN lines significantly increase the speed and quality of telecommunications (compared to standard telephone lines).

What does ISDN stand for?

    A   Integrated Services Digital Network
    B   International Systems Digital Network
    C   Integrated Services Dial-up Network
    D   International Systems Data Network

37   Which of the following input technologies uses a stylised font in banking applications?

    A   OMR
    B   OCR
    C   MICR
    D   BACS

38   Bits and bytes are terms used to describe the size of computer memory and storage. Which of the following statements is true?

    A   A bit is larger than a byte
    B   A byte is larger than a bit
    C   A byte is the same size as a bit
    D   A bit may be larger or smaller than a byte

Do you know? – Computer skills

Check that you can fill in the blanks in the statements below before you attempt any questions. If in doubt, you should go back to Chapters 2 and 3 of your BPP Interactive Text and revise.

- If a computer or a peripheral fails to respond correctly, one simple check is to check all **c**......... are connected correctly.

- When a computer stops responding it is said to have 'locked-up'. Causes of lock-ups include; too many programs running, not enough **m**............ to support the running programs, corrupt files, hardware failure and viruses.

- **El**............ mail, or e-mail is used for communication within organisations and between organisations.

- The Internet is accessed via an **I**............ **S**............ **P**............ and a browser. Searches are done using a **s**............ **e**.............

- **W**............ are a useful source of information although care should be taken to ensure the information is provided by a reliable organisation.

- Word processing software, such as Microsoft **W**............, is used to produce text-based documents such as letters, memos and reports.

- A spreadsheet is basically an electronic piece of paper divided into **r**......... and **c**............. The intersection of a row and a column is known as a **c**.......

- Essential basic skills include how to move around within a spreadsheet, how to enter and edit data, how to fill cells and how to **i**............ and **d**............ columns and rows.

- A spreadsheet should be given a **t**......... which clearly defines its purpose. The contents of rows and columns should also be clearly **l**.............

- Numbers can be **f**............ in several ways, for instance with commas, as percentages, as currency or with a certain number of decimal places.

- **R**............ cell references (B3) change when you copy formulae to other locations or move data from one place to another. **A**............ cell references (B3) stay the same.

- Spreadsheets can be **l**............ to, and exchange data with, word processing documents – and vice versa.

- Spreadsheets can be used in a variety of accounting contexts. You should practise using spreadsheets, **h**.........– **o**... experience is the key to spreadsheet proficiency.

TRY QUESTIONS 39 TO 80

- *Possible pitfalls. Write down examples of mistakes you should avoid.*

    –

    –

    –

    –

Did you know? – Computer skills

Could you fill in the blanks? The answers are in bold. Use this page for revision purposes as you approach the exam.

- If a computer or a peripheral fails to respond correctly, one simple check is to check all **cables** are connected correctly.

- When a computer stops responding it is said to have 'locked-up'. Causes of lock-ups include; too many programs running, not enough **memory** to support the running programs, corrupt files, hardware failure and viruses.

- **Electronic mail**, or e-mail is used for communication within organisations and between organisations.

- The Internet is accessed via an **Internet Service Provider** and a browser. Searches are done using a **search engine**.

- **Websites** are a useful source of information although care should be taken to ensure the information is provided by a reliable organisation.

- Word processing software, such as Microsoft **Word**, is used to produce text-based documents such as letters, memos and reports.

- A spreadsheet is basically an electronic piece of paper divided into **rows** and **columns**. The intersection of a row and a column is known as a **cell**.

- Essential basic skills include how to move around within a spreadsheet, how to enter and edit data, how to fill cells and how to **insert** and **delete** columns and rows.

- A spreadsheet should be given a **title** which clearly defines its purpose. The contents of rows and columns should also be clearly **labelled**.

- Numbers can be **formatted** in several ways, for instance with commas, as percentages, as currency or with a certain number of decimal places.

- **Relative** cell references (B3) change when you copy formulae to other locations or move data from one place to another. **Absolute** cell references (B3) stay the same.

- Spreadsheets can be **linked** to, and exchange data with, word processing documents – and vice versa.

- Spreadsheets can be used in a variety of accounting contexts. You should practise using spreadsheets, **hands-on** experience is the key to spreadsheet proficiency.

TRY QUESTIONS 39 TO 80

- *Possible pitfalls include the following (you may have thought of others).*

  - **Being unable to perform basic checks of cables and connections.**
  - **Insuffient time spent hands-on working with computers.**
  - **Failing to learn and understand the workings of spreadsheets.**
  - **Insufficient knowledge of appropriate formatting techniques.**

Objective test questions 39–80: Computer skills

39 Which of the following is **not** considered an advantage of e-mail?

A Secure method of communication
B Speedy delivery
C Stores messages for a given period after they are received
D Can make a single message available to many persons

40 Which of the following is **not** a typical function of an operating system?

A Booting
B Translating a program from one language to another
C Managing multi-tasking
D File management

Data for questions 41-43

You have acquired a spreadsheet package, Excel. You want to use it to devise a monthly schedule of your firm's income and expenditure over the past three months, in a format as shown below. The schedule is to be updated every month. (At the end of July, for example, the months shown will be July, June and May.) You decide that columns should represent months, with one to contain 'year-to-date' totals and each row should represent an item of income or expenditure, with a final profit figure at the bottom of each column, as in the illustration below. You also want to list the amount owing to your firm by its clients at the end of each month.

	A	B	C	D	E
1	Item	Total 3	June	May	April
2		months			
3		$	$	$	$
4	Fees		21500	22000	22500
5					
6					
7	Salaries		13500	12500	12500
8	Postage		200	200	200
9	Telephone		200	200	200
10	Stationery		200	200	200
11	Rent		1500	1500	1500
12	Accountancy		300	200	
13	Bank charges		–	400	
14	Rates		600	600	600
15	Other		1000	1200	1300
16					
17	Net		4000	5000	6000
18					
19	Owed by clients		7170	10995	9000
20					
21					
22					
23					

41 What should you enter in cell B4 when you construct the model, to make **best** use of the spreadsheet's facilities?

    A   66000
    B   =21500 + 22000 + 22500
    C   =SUM(C4:E4)
    D   =(C:E)*4

42 In Microsoft Excel, which **one** of the following would **not** correctly perform the calculation required in cell B17 (assuming the remainder of the spreadsheet is complete)?

    A   =B4-SUM(B7:B15)
    B   =SUM(C17:E17)
    C   B4-B7-B8-B9-B10-B11-B12-B13-B14-B15
    D   =SUM(C4:E4)-SUM(C7:E16)

43 You now wish to make your model more sophisticated, to include various items of a statistical nature. (1) The percentage change in revenue month by month is required. (2) The outstanding debt at the end of each month to be expressed as a proportion of the average daily revenue per month (assume each month has 30 days). Which of the following alternatives best expresses how you would input these requirements to your spreadsheet?

    A   (1): =(C4-D4)/D4 formatted as a percentage
            (2): =C19/(C4/30)

    B   (1): =C4-D4/D4 formatted as a percentage
            (2): =C19/C4/30

    C   (1): =C4-D4/D4 formatted as a percentage
            (2): =C19/C4/30

    D   (1): =C4-D4/D4 formatted as a percentage
            (2): =C19/(C4/30)

44 Which would be the fastest way to transmit a document from London to New York?

    A   Post
    B   Fax
    C   E-mail
    D   Courier (eg Fed Ex)

45 Which one of the following statements explaining examples of the advantages that a computer-based accounting system has over a manual system is **false**?

    A   A computer-based accounting system is easier to update as new information becomes available

    B   A computer-based accounting system will always reject inaccurate financial information input to the system

    C   Financial calculations can be performed more quickly and accurately

    D   The management accountant can more readily present financial information to other business departments in a variety of forms

46   Which one of the following statements is **incorrect**?

A   A help function is often a feature of a user-friendly program

B   A mouse-driven program can use both keyboard and mouse as input devices

C   Function keys on a keyboard enable the user to enter instructions quickly to the computer, in order to carry out defined operations with an application program

D   Icons are normally used on systems that do not need a mouse for input

47   Which of the following statements, referring to the Internet, are **correct**?

(i)   The Internet is owned by the United States government which controls standards on the system.

(ii)   The Internet is viewed through a browser.

(iii)   The Internet provides a completely secure system for all business communications.

(iv)   The Internet enables businesses to use electronic mail (e-mail) to communicate with suppliers and customers.

A   (i), (ii) and (iv) only
B   (ii) and (iii) only
C   (ii) and (iv) only
D   (i), (iii) and (iv) only

48   Which **one** of the following tasks is a spreadsheet **not** able to perform?

A   The presentation of numerical data in the form of graphs and charts
B   The application of logical tests to data
C   The application of 'What If' scenarios
D   Automatic correction of all data entered by the operator into the spreadsheet

49   All the following statements relate to computer communications systems.

(i)   Software applications known as 'search engines' have been developed to enable a computer user to locate information on the Internet.

(ii)   Computers can now communicate with each other by making use of satellite and fibre optic technology.

(iii)   Improvements in communications systems have facilitated the growth of teleworking and the emergence of the virtual organisation.

(iv)   External or built-in modems are always needed to enable networked computers to communicate with each other.

Which of the above statements are **correct**?

A   (i), (ii) and (iv) only
B   (ii) and (iii) only
C   (i), (ii) and (iii) only
D   (ii), (iii) and (iv) only

50   Spreadsheets are a well-known type of software application. All the following statements about spreadsheets are true expect one. Which **one** of the statements is **untrue**?

A   Spreadsheets can import information from documents created in other applications
B   Microsoft Access is a more advanced spreadsheet package than Microsoft Excel
C   It is possible to use a spreadsheet to sort data in a variety of ways
D   Spreadsheet packages usually include a facility to graph numeric data

51   The following statements are about word-processing software.

(i)   Standard word-processing applications can be used to check spelling and undertake a word count in a document.

(ii)   Standard word-processing applications automatically correct grammatical mistakes made by the user.

(iii)   Modern word-processing applications can import information produced on other applications such as databases and spreadsheets.

(iv)   A document produced on a word-processing application such as *Word* can be saved as a document in the format of another word-processing application such as *WordPerfect*.

Which of the above are correct?

A   (i) and (iii) only
B   (i) and (ii) only
C   (i) (iii) and (iv) only
D   (ii), (iii) and (iv) only

52   Which one of the following statements relating to the Internet is **false**?

A   Some of the information available on the Internet is poor quality

B   All business communication via the Internet is secured by the standards developed by Electronic Data Interchange (EDI) communication system

C   Some of the information on the Internet is high quality

D   Many businesses now include a website on the Internet as an element in their marketing mix

53   Which **one** of the following is **not** present on a typical PC keyboard?

A   Function keys
B   Escape
C   Total
D   Enter

54   Which **one** of the following is **not** an Internet Service Provider?

A   VirginNet
B   Intel
C   Freeserve
D   AOL

Questions 55-57 refer to the spreadsheet shown below.

	A	C	D	E	F	G	H	I
1			Income and Costs forecast for Smith and Peters					
2								
3			Month 1	Month 2	Month 3	Month 4	Month 5	Month 6
4			£	£	£	£	£	£
5	Opening position		0	1,430	2,860	4,290	5,720	7,150
6								
7	Income		15,000	15,000	15,000	15,000	15,000	15,000
8								
9	Costs							
10	Staff costs							
11	Project Manager		2,500	2,500	2,500	2,500	2,500	2,500
12	Senior Developer		1,900	1,900	1,900	1,900	1,900	1,900
13	Developer 1		1,600	1,600	1,600	1,600	1,600	1,600
14	Developer 2		1,500	1,500	1,500	1,500	1,500	1,500
15	Developer 3		1,500	1,500	1,500	1,500	1,500	1,500
16	Support Staff		1,200	1,200	1,200	1,200	1,200	1,200
17	National insurance @	10%	1,020	1,020	1,020	1,020	1,020	1,020
18	Total staff costs		11,220	11,220	11,220	11,220	11,220	11,220
19								
20	Insurances		50	50	50	50	50	50
21	Telephone, Telecom		250	250	250	250	250	250
22	Hardware/Software		500	500	500	500	500	500
23	Rent		800	800	800	800	800	800
24	Stationery		100	100	100	100	100	100
25	Accounting		300	300	300	300	300	300
26	Marketing		100	100	100	100	100	100
27	Other costs		250	250	250	250	250	250
28	Total other costs		2,350	2,350	2,350	2,350	2,350	2,350
29								
30	Total costs		13,570	13,570	13,570	13,570	13,570	13,570
31								
32	End month position		1,430	2,860	4,290	5,720	7,150	8,580

55   The cell F5 (column F row 5) shows the opening position for month 3. The value in this cell is a formula.

Which of the following would not be a correct entry for this cell?

A   =E7-E30+D32
B   =E5+E7-E30
C   =E32
D   =2860

56   The formula in D17 (column D row 17) adds a percentage national insurance charge to the sub total of staff costs. Which of the formulae shown below would be the **best** formula for cell D17?

A   =SUM(D11:D16)*0.1
B   =SUM(D11:D16)*$C17
C   =SUM(D11:D16)*10%
D   =SUM(D11:D16)*C17

57   The cell D30 (column D row 30) shows the total costs. Which of the following is the **correct** formula for this cell?

     A   =D28+D18
     B   = SUM(D11:D28)
     C   = SUM(D7:D28)
     D   D18+D28

58   The data that can be entered onto a spreadsheet comprises which of the following?

     A   Text and numbers
     B   Formulae, text and numbers
     C   Numbers and formulae
     D   Text and formulae

59   Spelling and grammar checking is a feature of a word processing package. Which **one** of the following is **not** a spelling or grammar checking test?

     A   Checking all full stops are followed by at least one space
     B   Highlighting incorrectly spelt words and suggesting corrections
     C   Highlighting very long sentences
     D   Checking all values in tables add up correctly

60   What is the name of the group of software products that includes Word, Excel, Outlook, PowerPoint and Access?

     A   Lotus Symphony
     B   Microsoft Works
     C   Microsoft Windows
     D   Microsoft Office

61   Which of the following is not an Internet search engine?

     A   Microsoft Internet Explorer
     B   Yahoo!
     C   Ask Jeeves
     D   Google

62   The protocol for communication between the client and server on the World Wide Web is called http.

   What does http stand for?

     A   Home To The Page Protocol
     B   HyperText Transfer Protocol
     C   Hyperlink Transfer Technology Protocol
     D   Hypermedia Transfer Technology Protocol

63   A user wishes to send an e-mail message to a long list of recipients without each individual recipient seeing the names or the e-mail address of the other recipients. What e-mail facility would allow this?

     A   Carbon Copy (cc)
     B   Blind Carbon Copy (bcc)
     C   Reply to all
     D   None – it is not possible

Questions 64, 65, 66 and 67 refer to the Employment targets and bonuses spreadsheet shown below.

This spreadsheet shows the target sales for each employee (column C) and the amount that they actually sold (column D). The bonus value is calculated by subtracting the actual sales from the target sales. If the employee has failed to achieve their target level, then there is no bonus. The target figure for next month (column F) is calculated by multiplying the target figure by a defined growth rate (cell B15).

	A	B	C	D	E	F	G
1							
2	Employment targets and bonuses						
3							
4	Employee No		Target	Actual	Bonus	Next month	
5	345	Rianne	2,100.00	2,000.00	0.00	2,121.00	
6	567	Sian	4,300.00	4,400.00	100.00	4,343.00	
7	543	Claire	2,345.00	2,300.00	0.00	2,368.45	
8	231	Mark	5,680.00	5,600.00	0.00	5,736.80	
9	890	Danny	345.00	500.00	155.00	348.45	
10							
11			14,770.00	14,800.00		14,917.70	
12	Sales staff	5					
13	Income/staff	2,960					
14							
15	Growth rate	1.00%					

64   In the spreadsheet what is the formula in C11 (column C row 11)?

    A   =SUM(C5:C9)

    B   =TOTAL(C5:C9)

    C   =SUM(C5:C11)

    D   =TOTAL (C5:C9)

65   In the spreadsheet the figure in E5 (column E row 5) is calculated by subtracting the value in D5 (column d row 5) from the value in C5 (column C row 5). However, if the calculated value is negative, then the value returned in E5 is zero.

In the spreadsheet what is the formula in E5?

    A   =IF(D5-C5>0,D5-C5,0)

    B   =IF(C5-D5>0,C5-D5,0)

    C   =IF(C5-D5>0,0,D5-C5)

    D   =IF(D5-C5>0,0,D5-C5)

66   The value in cell B12 (column C row 12) is a formula. It shows how many sales people are in the spreadsheet.

In the spreadsheet what is the formula in B12?

A   =SUM(A5:A9)
B   =TOTAL(A5:A9)
C   =COUNT(A5:A9)
D   =CALCULATE(A5:A9)

67   The value in F5 (column F row 5) is calculated by C5 (column C row 5) by the growth value in B15 (column B row 15). the formula in F5 is then copied down to rows 6, 7, 8 and 9

What should the formula be in F5 to allow this to be done accurately and quickly?

A   =$C5+($C5*B15)
B   =C5+($C5*$B$15)
C   =$C5+($C$5*$B$15)
D   =$C5+($C5*$B15)

68   The following phrase is contained in a word processed document; 'David likes to right letters'. It contains a mistake, as right should really read write.

What is the most likely way of the author finding this error?

A   Check the document with the spellchecker contained in the word processing software
B   Check the document with the grammar checker contained in the word processing software
C   Ask a colleague to carefully proof-read the document and indicate any mistakes
D   Check the document with a document imaging system to identify incorrectly used words

69   The screen print below shows the Print options from a Windows application.

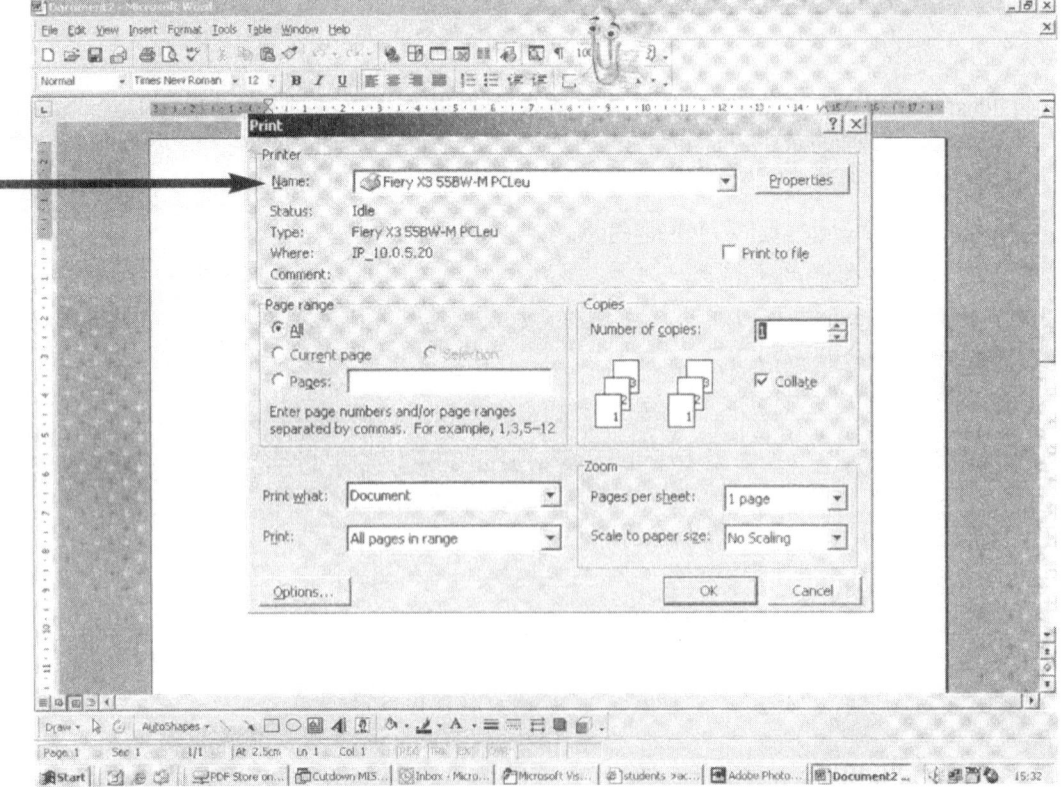

BPP
LEARNING MEDIA

Why does the field description <u>N</u>ame have the letter N underlined?

A   To emphasise the need for the user to check the name of the printer before printing

B   To allow the user to select the Name function using the ALT and N keys

C   To indicate that the printer name field is mandatory and hence should contain an entry

D   To indicate that the printer name field has a pull-down list of valid entries

---

70   The following formula is contained in a spreadsheet cell A3.

$$=(A1 + A2)^2$$

If the value in A1 is 1 and in A2 is 5, what is the value in A3?

A   12

B   36

C   26

D   2.45

---

71   The following formula is contained in a spreadsheet cell B5.

$$= ROUNDUP(B4,0)$$

If the value in B4 is 2.36, what is the value in B5?

A   3

B   2.5

C   2.4

D   0

---

72   With reference to the following screen, the user wishes to return to the page they viewed before this one.

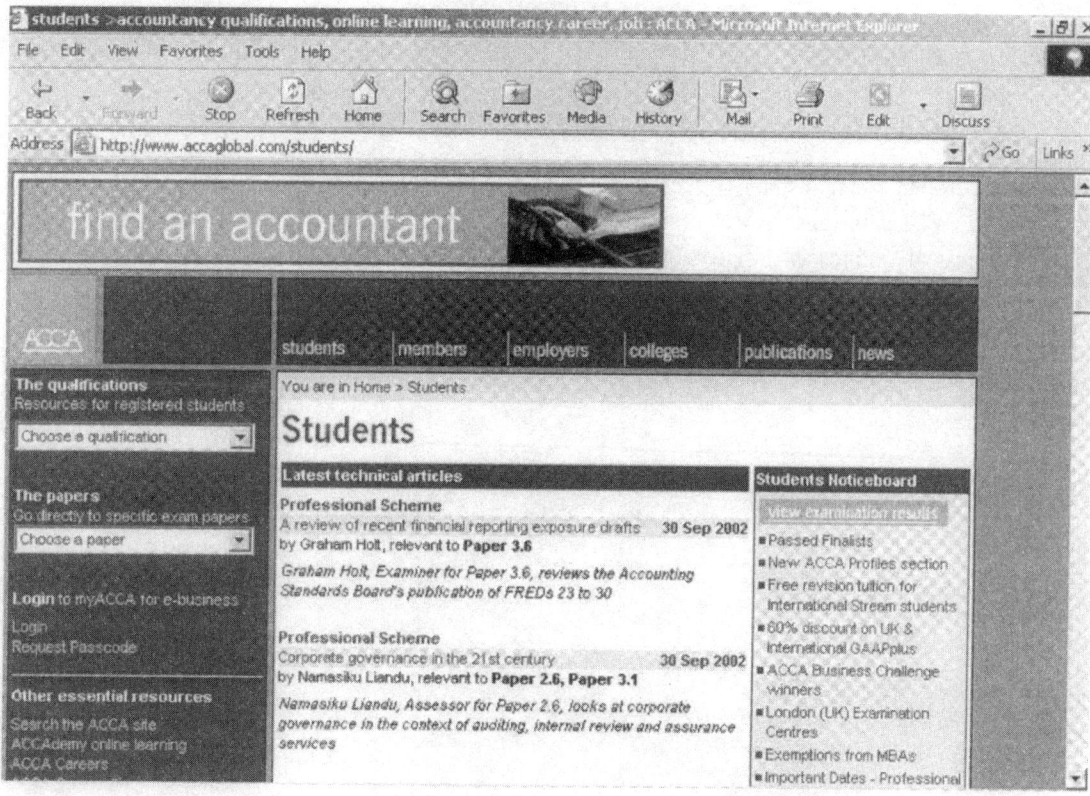

What command would they use?

A   Back
B   Refresh
C   History
D   Search

73   In the following screen the word Home is underlined (shown at the end of the large arrow).

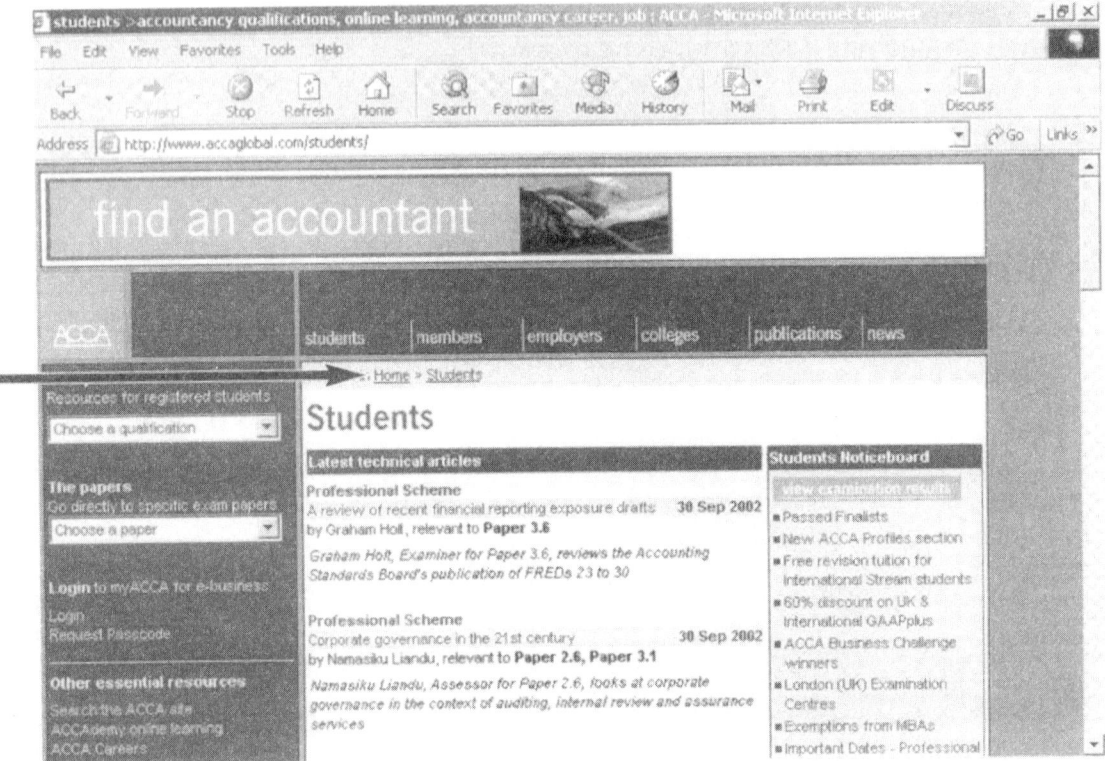

Why is the word Home underlined?

A   To indicate how important the Home page is to the user
B   To allow the user to select the Home function using the ALT and H keys
C   To allow the user to select this option through the Home page key on the keyboard
D   To indicate that it is a hypertext link to the Home page of the Internet site

Questions 74 to 77 refer to the following spreadsheet

	A	B	C	D	E	F	G
1							
2	Analysis of markers: Information Systems Development – 2003						
3							
4		Marker Code	Marker Name	Highest mark	Lowest mark	Range	Average
5							
6		1	Field	76	13	63	41.22
7		7	Warhurst	79	5	74	42
8		9	Singh	60	23	37	41.14
9		12	Lang	75	21	54	44
10		14	Yip	58	13	45	43.5
11		15	El Gerouge	75	15	60	45.4
12		17	Finley	69	30	39	50
13		19	Chen	87	32	55	46.4
14		23	Holmes	67	40	27	45.43
15		25	Chan	87	7	80	45.67
16		27	Cameron	90	30	60	42
17		29	Walsh	89	15	74	39
18		31	Menzies	70	20	50	43.7
19		32	Smith	70	9	61	43
20		35	Yonnie	67	30	37	43.7
21		36	Zammett	78	25	53	41.3
22		37	Caragher	70	30	40	43.6
23		38	O'Doyle	60	3	57	40
24		40	Blair	59	15	44	43.6
25		52	Craig	65	12	53	42.76
26							
27							
28	Number of markers		20				
29	Highest mark		90				
30	Lowest mark		3				

74   Column F shows the range between the highest and lowest marks for each marker. The value in cell F6 (column F row 6) is a formula. What is the likely formula in cell F6?

A   =E6–D6
B   =D6–E6
C   =76–13
D   =E6+D6

75   The cell C28 (column C row 28) shows the total number of markers who have marked this session. The value in cell C28 is a formula. What is the likely formula in cell C28?

A   = COUNT(C6:C25)
B   = COUNT(B6:B25)
C   = TOTAL(C6:C25)
D   = TOTAL(B6:B25)

76 The cell C29 (column C row 29) automatically shows the highest mark obtained in this session. The value in cell C29 is a formula. What is the likely formula in cell C29?

A   = MAX(D6:D25)
B   = HIGH(D6:D25)
C   = TOP(D6:D25)
D   = PEAK(D6:D25)

77 The examiner wishes to arrange the markers on the spreadsheet into descending order of average mark. Should the command used be DATA;

A   FILTER
B   FORM
C   TABLE
D   SORT

78 In the context of computing, what is USB?

A   A type of port and connection
B   A type of monitor
C   A new type of mouse that doesn't use a trackball
D   An ergonomic keyboard

79 Web browsers allow access to the World Wide Web. They read HTML files and display them as graphical documents. Which of the following is a Web Browser?

A   Google
B   Altavista
C   Microsoft Internet Explorer
D   Yahoo!

80 FTP is a standard for the transfer of files over the Internet. What does FTP stand for?

A   Faster Than Post
B   File Transfer Pentium
C   Forward This Please
D   File Transfer Protocol

Do you know? – Security, back-ups and legal issues

Check that you can fill in the blanks in the statements below before you attempt any questions. If in doubt, you should go back to Chapters 4 and 5 of your BPP Interactive Text and revise.

- There are many different risks in the IT environment, both to computer hardware and to the organisation's data. **H**............ **e**............ is probably the most common.

- Physical **a**............ **c**............ attempts to stop intruders or other unauthorised persons getting near to computer equipment or storage media.

- Computer **f**............ may involve the theft of stock (inventory), equipment, information or funds. The opportunities for people to commit fraud are growing as computers become more widespread and computer literacy increases.

- A **l**............ access system is concerned with preventing those persons who have gained physical access from gaining unauthorised access to data or software.

- When data is transmitted over telecommunications links, there are a number of security risks. One method of preventing eavesdropping is **e**..............., which scrambles up data while it is being transmitted.

- A **h**............ is a person who attempts to invade the privacy of a system by circumventing logical access controls. A **v**............ is a piece of software which corrupts the operation of programs.

- **P**.............. are a set of characters which are required to be keyed before access is permitted.

- Passwords should be kept safe and should not be revealed to other users. Passwords should be **c**............ regularly, or **i**.............. if disclosure is suspected.

- A **b**.........-**u**... copy of computer file(s) is a duplicate copy kept separately from the main system and only used if the original fails. If the back-up copy need to be used it is **r**............ to the system.

- Organisations should also have some back-up plan for their computer **h**..............., such as an arrangement that would allow appropriate alternative equipment to be used.

- The process of moving (by copying) data from primary storage, such as a hard disk, to tape or other portable media for long-term storage is known as **a**.............

- At least some back-ups should be stored **o**......-**s**..........

- The **D**...... **P**............ **A**...... aims to protect the rights of individuals in relation to information organisations hold about them.

TRY QUESTIONS 81 TO 100

- *Possible pitfalls. Write down examples of mistakes you should avoid.*

  –

  –

  –

  –

Did you know? – Security, back-ups and legal issues

Could you fill in the blanks? The answers are in bold. Use this page for revision purposes as you approach the exam.

- There are many different risks in the IT environment, both to computer hardware and to the organisation's data. **Human error** is probably the most common.

- Physical **access control** attempts to stop intruders or other unauthorised persons getting near to computer equipment or storage media.

- Computer **fraud** may involve the theft of stock (inventory), equipment, information or funds. The opportunities for people to commit fraud are growing as computers become more widespread and computer literacy increases.

- A **logical** access system is concerned with preventing those persons who have gained physical access from gaining unauthorised access to data or software.

- When data is transmitted over telecommunications links, there are a number of security risks. One method of preventing eavesdropping is **encryption**, which scrambles up data while it is being transmitted.

- A **hacker** is a person who attempts to invade the privacy of a system by circumventing logical access controls. A **virus** is a piece of software which corrupts the operation of programs.

- **Passwords** are a set of characters which are required to be keyed before access is permitted.

- Passwords should be kept safe and should not be revealed to other users. Passwords should be **changed** regularly, or **immediately** if disclosure is suspected.

- A **back-up** copy of computer file(s) is a duplicate copy kept separately from the main system and only used if the original fails. If the back-up copy need to be used it is **restored** to the system.

- Organisations should also have some back-up plan for their computer **hardware**, such as an arrangement that would allow appropriate alternative equipment to be used.

- The process of moving (by copying) data from primary storage, such as a hard disk, to tape or other portable media for long-term storage is known as **archiving**.

- At least some back-ups should be stored **off-site**.

- The **Data Protection Act** aims to protect the rights of individuals in relation to information organisations hold about them.

TRY QUESTIONS 81 TO 100

- *Possible pitfalls include the following (you may have thought of others).*

    - **Focusing solely on technical risks to computer systems and neglecting 'human' risks.**
    - **Not understanding the purpose and process of backing up and restoring.**
    - **Under-estimating the importance of appropriate password policies and procedures.**
    - **Not grasping the main aims of the Data Protection Act.**

Objective test questions 81-100: Security, back-ups and legal issues

81   Fast tape-units used to create back-up files are known as:

A   Tape writers
B   Tape spoolers
C   Tape streamers
D   Tape copiers

82   Two terms which relate to the use of codes to ensure controls over data transmission are encryption and authentication. Which of the following statements is correct?

A   Authentication ensures that the message goes to an authorised recipient by use of a commonly determined algorithm and encryption ensures that the message has come from an authorised source

B   Authentication is carried out to ensure that a message has been encrypted successfully

C   Authentication is the reassembly and decoding of an encrypted message

D   Encryption involves scrambling in cipher a message to prevent eavesdropping by third parties, and an authentication code is a check appended to a message to ensure that the message has not been tampered with

83   Which of the following statements is true? The Data Protection Act 1998 aims to protect:

A   Data about individuals
B   Manual and computer records relating to individuals
C   Only manually processed data relating to individuals
D   Only data relating to individuals processed by computer

84   A data protection officer is:

A   One of the Data Protection Registrar's deputies

B   Appointed by an organisation to ensure that it complies with the Data Protection Act 1998

C   An official whose job it is to ensure that the organisation's networks are safe from unauthorised access

D   An official in charge of an organisation's data archive

85   Which of the following is responsible for the implementation of the Data Protection Act?

A   Comptroller & Auditor General
B   Audit Commission
C   Data Protection Registrar
D   Department of Trade & Industry

86   A small company's computer system comprises five desktop personal computers located in separate offices linked together in a local area network within the same building. The computers are not connected to any external network and employees are not allowed to take floppy disks into or out of the building. Confidential information is stored on one of the computers. Which one of the following statements can be concluded from this information?

The company's computer system does not:

A   Need a back-up system
B   Need a password access system
C   Receive e-mail from customers or suppliers
D   Include virus detection software

87   The consequences of the activities of hackers can be very serious for an organisation. One from the list below is not a risk associated with hacking. Which one is it?

A   Generate information which is of potential use to a competitor
B   Provide the basis for fraudulent activity
C   Alter or delete the files
D   Steal computer hardware

88   A disaffected programmer has installed a malicious program into a computer system. This program will be invoked the next time that the payroll program is run. The malicious program will delete the main employee file of the payroll system.

What is this type of program known as?

A   Trap door
B   Logic bomb
C   Hoax
D   Worm

89   One way of securing transmitting data is to scramble it at the sender's end and then unscramble it at the receiver's end of the line. This scrambling makes the message meaningless to unauthorised users who do not have the necessary decoding mechanisms.

Which of the following is this an example of?

A   Data encryption
B   Data modulation, demodulation
C   Packet switching
D   Multiplexing

90   An organisation has a large customer data file stored on its computer system. The size of this file is one of the factors causing the computer systems in the organisation to perform inefficiently. A consultant has pointed out that almost half of the customers on the file have not ordered for five years and suggests that information about such customers should be moved to magnetic tapes for long-term storage.

Which of the following terms best describes the process of moving this data?

A   Backing-up
B   Archiving
C   Dumping
D   Defragmenting

91   In the United Kingdom, which Act covers issues relating to the accuracy and use of information organisations hold about individuals?

A   Computer Misuse Act
B   Data Protection Act
C   Computer Protection Act
D   Data Misuse Act

92   What is the abbreviation PIN short for?

    A   Primary Internal Node
    B   Personal Industry Number
    C   Prevent Intruder Number
    D   Personal Identification Number

93   The process of using back-up files to replace current, damaged files, is known as what?

    A   Restore
    B   Salvage
    C   Back date
    D   Cloning

94   Which **one** of the following statements is **true**?

    A   Bugs are often introduced by hackers
    B   Most computer software is 100% bug free
    C   Viruses spread most rapidly via floppy disks
    D   Hoax e-mails warning of viruses are more common than genuine virus warnings

95   The unlawful activity of attempting to gain unauthorised access to a computer system is commonly referred to as:

    A   Distorting
    B   Free-loading
    C   Hacking
    D   Zipping

96   Why should some computer back-ups be stored off-site?

    A   To save office space
    B   To enable working at home
    C   To conform with the procedures manual
    D   To ensure a back-up is available should the office be damaged or destroyed

97   Which **one** of the following security options is unlikely to be feasible for most businesses?

    A   Iris scanning
    B   After hours security guard
    C   Swipe card access
    D   Door access combination code

98   Which **one** of the following statements about passwords is **true**?

    A   If you have a password you know you won't forget, you should never change it
    B   You should change your password every day
    C   Your password should be easy for you to remember, but difficult for anyone else to guess
    D   You should make a note of your password and keep this in your desk drawer

99   Which **one** of the following is a type of anti-virus software?

    A   Raid
    B   Norton
    C   McAnally
    D   Novell

100   The most common cause of incorrect data in a computer system is:

    A   Hacking
    B   Viruses
    C   Hardware failure
    D   Human error

Do you know? – Introduction to management information and reporting management information

Check that you can fill in the blanks in the statements below before you attempt any questions. If in doubt, you should go back to your BPP Interactive Text and revise first.

- .... is processed to produce information.

- The purpose of management information is to help managers to manage resources efficiently and effectively by planning and ...., and to take ....

- Good management information has the following characteristics.

    - ....
    - ....
    - ....

- There are many sources of information for management accounting, some of which are shared with financial accounting. Computer systems and .... help to sort the information into the categories and formats required for both financial and management accounting.

- Regular reports are a regular part of the ....

- .... reports deal with a one-off issue or problem.

- Types of written communication include the following.

    - ....
    - ....
    - ....
    - ....

- Access to .... information will be restricted. This may be because of the Data Protection Act, or because of company policy. If you have access to restricted information, in whatever form, you are responsible for protecting it.

- Types of non-written communication include the following.

    - ....
    - ....
    - ....

TRY QUESTIONS 101 TO 120

- *Possible pitfalls. Write down examples of mistakes you should avoid.*

    -
    -
    -
    -

Did you know? – Introduction to management information and reporting management information

Could you fill in the blanks? The answers are in bold. Use this page for revision purposes as you approach the exam.

- **Data** is processed to produce information.

- The purpose of management information is to help managers to manage resources efficiently and effectively by planning and **control**, and to take **decisions**.

- Good management information has the following characteristics.

    - **Reliable**
    - **Timely**
    - **Relevant**

- There are many sources of information for management accounting, some of which are shared with financial accounting. Computer systems and **coding structures** help to sort the information into the categories and formats required for both financial and management accounting.

- Regular reports are a regular part of the **management information system**.

- **Ad-hoc** reports deal with a one-off issue or problem.

- Types of written communication include the following.

    - **Letters**
    - **Memos**
    - **E-mails**
    - **Formal reports**

- Access to **confidential** information will be restricted. This may be because of the Data Protection Act, or because of company policy. If you have access to restricted information, in whatever form, you are responsible for protecting it.

- Types of non-written communication include the following.

    - **Charts**
    - **Graphs**
    - **Tables**

TRY QUESTIONS 101 TO 120

- *Possible pitfalls include the following (you may have thought of others)*

    - **Not being able to distinguish between data and information**
    - **Not being able to describe the features of useful management information**
    - **Not being able to distinguish between management accounts and financial accounts**
    - **Not having a clear picture of the accounting technician's role in a cost accounting system**

Objective test questions 101-120: Introduction to management information and reporting management information

101   How would facts and figures which have been processed and communicated to another party be best described?

    A   Data
    B   Statistics
    C   Information
    D   Coding

102   Which of the following would be data rather than information?

    A   Sales increase/decrease per product in last quarter
    B   Total sales value per product
    C   Sales made per salesman as a percentage of total sales
    D   Salesmens' commission as a percentage of total sales

103   Two statements follow about data and information:

    1   Data is a scientific term for facts, figures and information
    2   Information is data which has been processed

Which one of the following is correct with regard to the above two statements?

    A   Both statements are false
    B   Both statements are true
    C   Statement 1 is true but statement 2 is false
    D   Statement 1 is false but statement 2 is true

104   Which of the following combinations describe the purposes of management information?

    A   Planning, negotiating and decision making
    B   Control, decision making and publication
    C   Decision making, negotiating and implementing
    D   Planning, control and decision making

105   The cost accountant has produced a report showing the hourly output from the factory floor for the last week. Who in the organisation is most likely to require this information?

    A   The financial accountant
    B   The sales director
    C   The production manager
    D   The human resources manager

106   Which of the following is not a quality of good management information?

    A   Clarity
    B   Reliability
    C   Accuracy
    D   Computerised

107 The cost accountant has provided information about the actual and budgeted cost of the materials used in production in the last month. This information will primarily aid management in which of the following areas?

    A   Planning
    B   Implementing
    C   Control
    D   Decision making

108 Which of the following is not an example of internal information for the accounts department?

    A   Goods received note
    B   Time sheets for employees
    C   Materials requisitions from the factory
    D   Purchase invoices from suppliers

109 Three statements follow about management accounting:

    1   Management accounts are a legal requirement for a company
    2   Management accounts consider future data only
    3   Management accounts include financial and non-financial information

Which of the statements above are true?

    A   1 and 3 only
    B   2 and 3 only
    C   2 only
    D   3 only

110 Which of the following is not an attribute of management accounts?

    A   Based on historical data only
    B   Produced for internal use only
    C   Used for planning, decision making and control
    D   Presented according to management's wishes

111 Which of the following could be considered to be a limitation of cost and management accounting information?

    A   Affected by changing prices over time
    B   Includes non-financial as well as financial information
    C   Produced periodically
    D   Produced in the format required by management

112 When communicating information, which of the following combinations of factors would influence the method of communication used?

    1   Timeliness
    2   Confidentiality
    3   Complexity

    A   All three
    B   1 and 2 only
    C   1 and 3 only
    D   2 and 3 only

113 If a letter is started with the greeting 'Dear Mr Smith', how should the letter be signed?

A   Yours truly
B   Yours sincerely
C   Yours faithfully
D   Yours gratefully

114 Two statements follow about the use of e-mail as a form of communication:

1   E-mail can be used for confidential information
2   E-mail should not be used where a signature is necessary

Which one of the following is correct with regard to the above statements?

A   Both statements are false
B   Both statements are true
C   Statement 1 is true but statement 2 is false
D   Statement 1 is false but statement 2 is true

115 A complaint is to be made to a supplier about quality and reliability of the goods supplied. Which is the most appropriate form of communication?

A   Memo
B   E-mail
C   Letter
D   Report

116 If a company wishes to hold personal data in a permanent form for a particular purpose to whom must the company apply?

A   The Department of Trade and Industry
B   Companies House
C   Data Protection Registrar
D   Local authority

117 Which of the following is true about a line graph?

A   The independent variable is always shown on the y axis
B   The independent variable is always shown on the x axis
C   The dependent variable is always shown on the x axis
D   It does not matter on which axis each variable is shown

118 Information about the trend in monthly sales and profit for a product for the last two years is to be presented visually. Which would be the most appropriate method of presentation?

A   Pie chart
B   Bar chart
C   Table
D   Line graph

119 A visual method of presenting the percentage of total sales for the last year made by each of a company's ten divisions is required. Which of the following would be the most appropriate method?

A   Pie chart
B   Bar chart
C   Line graph
D   Spreadsheet

120 A colleague asks you for your computer password in order to access supplier information which he does not normally deal with. He explains that this is in order to produce a special report for the management accountant. What should you do?

    A   Give your password to your colleague

    B   Access the information yourself and print it out for your colleague

    C   Give your password to your colleague on this occasion and then change your password

    D   Refer the query to the management accountant

Do you know? – Business organisation and accounting

Check that you can fill in the blanks in the statements below before you attempt any questions. If in doubt, you should go back to your BPP Interactive Text and revise first.

- The office in an organisation is a centre for information and administration. The most common functions in an office are as follows.

    – ....
    – Personnel (.................... ....)
    – ....
    – ....
    – ....

- A .... should help to ensure that all personnel follow procedures and best practices.

- The main types of transactions that most businesses enter into are sales, purchases, paying expenses, paying employees and purchasing fixed assets. In order for management to control the transactions of the business there must be a system of .... of transactions in place.

- The basic principle of .... is that for every debit entry there must be a corresponding credit entry.

- Increases in assets or expenses and decreases in liabilities and income are .... entries in ledger accounts.

- Increases in liabilities and income and decreases in assets and expenses are .... entries in ledger accounts.

- Transactions are initially recorded in books of .... which are totalled and the totals posted to the ledger accounts.

- A system in which the cost accounting and financial accounting functions are combined in one system of ledger accounts is known as an .... system.

- A system in which there is a cost ledger for the cost accounting function and a financial ledger for the financial accounting function is known as an .... system.

- Computerised accounting systems allow much quicker and more accurate entries to the accounting system.

TRY QUESTIONS 121 TO 130

- *Possible pitfalls. Write down examples of mistakes you should avoid.*

    –
    –
    –
    –

Did you know? – Business organisation and accounting

Could you fill in the blanks? The answers are in bold. Use this page for revision purposes as you approach the exam.

- The office in an organisation is a centre for information and administration. The most common functions in an office are as follows.

  - **Purchasing**
  - Personnel (**human resources**)
  - **General administration**
  - **Finance**
  - **Sales and marketing**

- A **policy manual** should help to ensure that all personnel follow procedures and best practices.

- The main types of transactions that most businesses enter into are sales, purchases, paying expenses, paying employees and purchasing fixed assets. In order for management to control the transactions of the business there must be a system of **authorisation** of transactions in places.

- The basic principle of **double entry bookkeeping** is that for every debit entry there must be a corresponding credit entry.

- Increases in assets or expenses and decreases in liabilities and income are **debit** entries in ledger accounts.

- Increases in liabilities and income and decreases in assets and expenses are **credit** entries in ledger accounts.

- Transactions are initially recorded in books of **prime entry** which are totalled and the totals posted to the ledger accounts.

- A system in which the cost accounting and financial accounting functions are combined in one system of ledger accounts is known as an **integrated system**.

- A system in which there is a cost ledger for the cost accounting function and a financial ledger for the financial accounting function is known as an **interlocking** system.

- Computerised accounting systems allow much quicker and more accurate entries to the accounting system.

TRY QUESTIONS 121 TO 130

- *Possible pitfalls include the following (you may have thought of others).*

  - **Not understanding the principles of double entry bookkeeping**
  - **Not being able to distinguish between integrated and interlocking accounting systems**
  - **Not being able to explain the concept of cost centres/profit centres/investment centres**
  - **Not being able to apply performance measures appropriate to cost, profit and investment**

Objective test questions 121–130: Business organisation and accounting

121 Which of the following will not be a function of the human resources department?

A   Hiring employees
B   Firing employees
C   Paying employees
D   Arranging training of employees

122 The following statements relate to the policy manual of an organisation:

1   Policies should be in place to deal with the authorisation of the purchase of fixed assets
2   Employees will need to know where to find the policy manual to refer to but need not have read it
3   Strict adherence to the manual can lead to inflexibility

A   All three
B   1 and 2 only
C   1 and 3 only
D   2 and 3 only

123 Which of the following documents is not part of the purchasing system?

A   Purchase requisition
B   Goods received note
C   Despatch note
D   Purchase invoice

124 Which of the following personnel in an organisation would not be involved in the sale of goods on credit?

A   Stores manager
B   Purchase ledger controller
C   Credit controller
D   Accountant

125 What is the double entry for a purchase of goods on credit?

A   Debit   Creditors (payables)
    Credit Purchases

B   Debit   Debtors (receivables)
    Credit Purchases

C   Debit   Purchases
    Credit Creditors (payables)

D   Debit   Purchases
    Credit Debtors (receivables)

126 What is the double entry for materials returned to a supplier which had been purchased on credit?

   A   Debit Creditors (payables)
          Credit Purchases returns

   B   Debit Debtors (receivables)
          Credit Purchases returns

   C   Debit Purchases returns
          Credit Creditors (payables)

   D   Debit Purchases returns
          Credit Debtors (receivables)

127 The following statements relate to the recording of accounting transactions in books of prime entry:

1 Credit notes from suppliers are recorded in the sales returns day book
2 Invoices to customers are recorded in the sales day book
3 Payments for expenses are recorded in the cash payments book

Which of the statements above are true?

   A   1 and 2 only
   B   1 and 3 only
   C   2 and 3 only
   D   All three

128 The following statements relate to cost ledger accounting:

1 An integrated system is one where separate ledgers are kept for cost accounting and management accounting

2 An interlocking system is one where there is just one system of ledger accounts for cost accounting and for management accounting

Which of the following is correct with regard to the above statements?

   A   Both statements are correct
   B   Neither statement is correct
   C   Statement 1 is correct but statement 2 is incorrect
   D   Statement 2 is correct but statement 1 is incorrect

129 Which of the following describes the cost ledger control account?

   A   An account which can be used to reconcile creditor (supplier) balances
   B   An account which can be used to reconcile debtor (customer) balances
   C   An account in the cost ledger to record financial items
   D   An account in the financial ledger to record costing items

130 Purchase invoices are entered into an organisation's computer system at the end of each day. What is this an example of?

   A   Batch processing
   B   Real time on line processing
   C   File maintenance
   D   File updating

Do you know? – Management responsibility and performance measurement; cost units, cost classification and profit reporting

Check that you can fill in the blanks in the statements below before you attempt any questions. If in doubt, you should go back to your BPP Interactive Text and revise first.

- A function or department of an organisation that is headed by a manager who has direct responsibility for its performance is known as a(n) .... centre.

- A unit of an organisation to which costs can be separately attributed is known as a(n) ...... centre.

- A unit of an organisation to which both revenues and costs are assigned is known as a profit centre. A profit centre whose performance is measured by its return on capital employed is known as a(n) .... centre.

- Performance measurement aims to establish how well something or somebody is doing in relation to a planned activity. Useful performance measurement techniques are as follows.

    - ....…..
    - ....

- Total costs ÷ number of units produced = ...

- The profit margin (profit to sales ratio) is calculated as (X ÷ Y) × 100% where:

    X = ...
    Y = ...

- The amount of profit made in relation to the amount of resources invested is known as the .... or ....

- Residual income also measures the performance of an investment centre. It measures the centre's profits after deducting a .... interest cost.

- A unit of product which has costs attached to it is known as a ....

- The ways in which costs are affected by changes in the level of activity are known as ....

- Costs which are fixed in nature within certain levels of activity are known as ....-......... costs.

- Semi-variable/semi-fixed costs are partly fixed and partly variable and therefore only partly affected by changes in activity levels. They are also known as .... costs.

- Costs can also be analysed according to their ...., for example, production, distribution and selling, administration and financing costs.

TRY QUESTIONS 131 TO 169

- *Possible pitfalls. Write down examples of mistakes you should avoid.*

    -
    -
    -
    -

Did you know? – Management responsibility and performance measurement; cost units, cost classification and profit reporting

Could you fill in the blanks? The answers are in bold. Use this page for revision purposes as you approach the exam.

- A function or department of an organisation that is headed by a manager who has direct responsibility for its performance is known as a(n) **responsibility** centre.

- A unit of an organisation to which costs can be separately attributed is known as a(n) **cost** centre.

- A unit of an organisation to which both revenues and costs are assigned is known as a profit centre. A profit centre whose performance is measured by its return on capital employed is known as a(n) **investment** centre.

- Performance measurement aims to establish how well something or somebody is doing in relation to a planned activity. Useful performance measurement techniques are as follows.

  - **Ratios**
  - **Percentages**

- Total costs ÷ number of units produced = **cost per unit**.

- The profit margin (profit to sales ratio) is calculated as $(X \div Y) \times 100\%$ where:

  X = **profit**
  Y = **sales**

- The amount of profit made in relation to the amount of resources invested is known as the **return on investment** or **return on capital employed**.

- Residual income also measures the performance of an investment centre. It measures the centre's profits after deducting a **notional** interest cost.

- A unit of product which has costs attached to it is known as a **cost unit**.

- The ways in which costs are affected by changes in the level of activity are known as **cost behaviour patterns**.

- Costs which are fixed in nature within certain levels of activity are known as **stepped-fixed** costs.

- Semi-variable/semi-fixed costs are partly fixed and partly variable and therefore only partly affected by changes in activity levels. They are also known as **mixed** costs.

- Costs can also be analysed according to their **function**, for example, production, distribution and selling, administration and financing costs.

TRY QUESTIONS 131 TO 169

- *Possible pitfalls include the following (you may have thought of others).*

  - **Not being able to describe the variety of cost classifications used for different purposes**
  - **Not being able to illustrate the nature of variable, fixed and mixed costs**
  - **Not being able to prepare profit statements in absorption and marginal costing formats**
  - **Not being able to calculate the cost of a product or service**

Objective test questions 131-169: Management responsibility and performance measurement; cost units, cost classification and profit reporting

131 Which is the best description of responsibility accounting?

A Employees will be held responsible for all decisions they make
B Managers delegate responsibility for performance to employees
C Directors delegate responsibility for performance to managers
D Managers bear responsibility for the revenues and costs of their area of the business

132 The following statements relate to responsibility accounting:

1 Managers are held responsible for all costs incurred by their cost centre
2 Shared costs should be apportioned between the cost centres that incur them
3 Cost centre costs will be collected by allocating a cost code to the cost

Which of the statements above are correct?

A 1 and 2 only
B 1 and 3 only
C 2 and 3 only
D All three

133 A manager has responsibility for both costs incurred and revenues earned by his area of the business.

This means that the manager is responsible for which one of the following?

A A cost centre
B A revenue centre
C A profit centre
D An investment centre

134 A manager in a division has his performance measured on the basis of the amount of profit the division makes in relation to the capital invested in the division.

Which of the following is the manager responsible for?

A A cost centre
B A revenue centre
C A profit centre
D An investment centre

135 A manufacturing company produces a range of goods which it manufactures and sells around the country, some sales being for cash and some on credit. The management are considering the closure of some of the manufacturing and selling outlets.

How might the company best analyse its results for this purpose?

A Sales per outlet
B Sales in each area of the country
C Profitability per outlet
D Profitability in each area of the country

136 Which of the following would not be a measure of productivity in a manufacturing organisation?

  A   Cost per unit of production
  B   Production per employee
  C   Production per hour
  D   Units produced per kilogram of materials

137 In May a manufacturing company produced 150,200 units of its single product and in June 183,300 units. The manufacturing costs incurred in June were $67,821 and in May were $51,068.

  What was the increase (in cents) in cost per unit?

  A   3c increase
  B   11c increase
  C   17c increase
  D   51c increase

138 A material that a company uses in its production has cost the following amounts on average each year for the last four years:

  20X0 $15.00
  20X1 $15.50
  20X2 $16.10
  20X3 $16.70

  Using 20X0 as the base year (ie 100), what is the index value of the 20X3 price (to one decimal place)?

  A   89.8
  B   103.3
  C   107.3
  D   111.3

139 The standard production per employee of a company's single product is 10 units per hour. During week 14 the factory produced 6,200 units of the product. 15 employees worked for an average of 40 hours each during the week.

  What is the index value of the actual production compared to that of standard production (to one decimal place)?

  A   96.7
  B   100.0
  C   103.3
  D   150.0

140 A business has credit sales of $150,000 and cash sales of $50,000. The production costs are $120,000 with selling costs of $35,000 and administration costs of $25,000.

  What is the gross profit margin (to the nearest one decimal place)?

  A   10.0%
  B   20.0%
  C   22.5%
  D   40.0%

141 A business has credit sales of $150,000 and cash sales of $50,000. The production costs are $120,000 with selling costs of $35,000 and administration costs of $25,000.

What is the operating profit margin (to the nearest one decimal place)?

A   10.0%
B   20.0%
C   22.5%
D   40.0%

142 You are given the following information about a business.

Gross profit margin   30%
Gross profit $240,000
Operating expenses $106,000

What is the operating profit margin (to two decimal places)?

A   14.72%
B   16.75%
C   33.97%
D   55.83%

143 A manufacturer makes three very different products, the A, B and C. The standard time allowed for each unit of each product is as follows.

A   1 hour
B   1.5 hours
C   1.75 hours

During April, 2,000 units of A were made, 800 units of B and 1,400 units of C.

What are the standard hours of output for April?

A   2,000 standard hours
B   3,200 standard hours
C   4,200 standard hours
D   5,650 standard hours

144 What are the three labour control ratios?

A   Efficiency, capacity utilisation, production volume
B   Rate, efficiency, capacity
C   Rate, idle time, production volume
D   Capacity, idle time, efficiency

145 During quarter 2 a manufacturing business had budgeted for 12,000 labour hours to be worked. The actual hours worked were 11,400 and the standard hours of production were 10,800.

What is the labour efficiency ratio (to one decimal place)?

A   90.0%
B   94.7%
C   95.0%
D   105.6%

146   During quarter 2, a manufacturing business had budgeted for 12,000 labour hours to be worked. The actual hours worked were 11,400 and the standard hours of production were 10,800.

What is the labour capacity ratio (to one decimal place)?

A   90.0%
B   94.7%
C   95.0%
D   105.6%

147   During quarter 2, a manufacturing business had budgeted for 12,000 labour hours to be worked. The actual hours worked were 11,400 and the standard hours of production were 10,800.

What is the labour activity ratio (to one decimal place)?

A   90.0%
B   94.7%
C   95.0%
D   105.6%

148   Which of the following is the best description of residual income?

A   Profits after interest and tax but before depreciation
B   Profit before interest, tax and depreciation
C   Profit before tax less a notional interest charge
D   Profit after tax, interest and depreciation

149   An investment centre has fixed assets with a value of $300,000 and net current assets totalling $40,000 as at 31 December 20X3. It made a profit before tax of $40,000 and the tax charge for the year was $10,000.

What is the return on investment for the investment centre for the year (to one decimal place)?

A   8.8%
B   11.5%
C   11.8%
D   15.4%

150   Which of the following would not be a cost unit in a hospital?

A   Patient night
B   Ward bed
C   X-Ray department
D   Canteen meal

151   Which of the following is the best description of a direct cost?

A   A cost which is directly shared by one or more cost centres
B   A cost that can be directly traced to a cost unit
C   A cost that is paid for in cash
D   A cost that is incurred by the factory

152   Which of the following is most likely to be treated as an indirect cost by a car manufacturer?

A   Sheet metal for car body
B   Wages of factory workers
C   Lubricant for machinery
D   Fabric for car seats

153 Which of the following is most likely to be treated as an indirect cost by a computer manufacturer?

A   Factory worker wages
B   Microchips
C   Plastic housing for computer bodies
D   Factory supervisor's wages

154 Which of the following costs would be most likely to be illustrated by the cost curve given below?

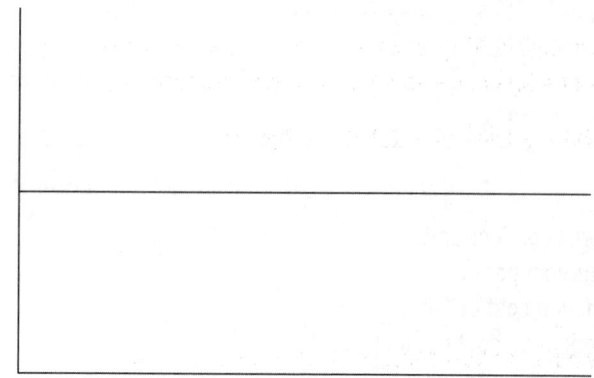

A   Total materials cost
B   Factory rent
C   Total wages cost
D   Telephone expense

155 Which description best fits the cost curve shown below?

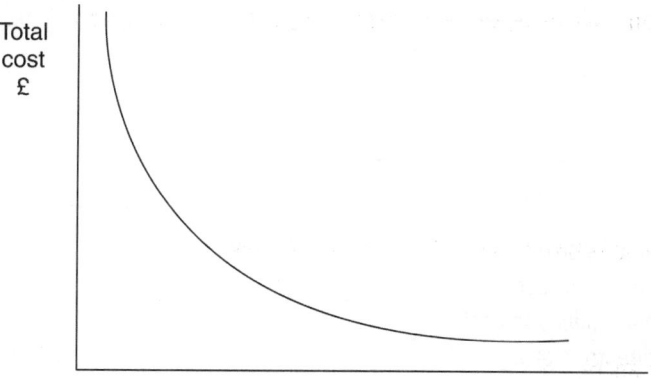

A   Direct material cost per unit
B   Direct labour cost per unit
C   Variable production cost per unit
D   Fixed production cost per unit

156 Which of the following is the best description of a stepped-fixed cost?

A   A cost with both a fixed element and a variable element
B   A cost which increases as the level of activity increases
C   A cost which is fixed no matter what the level of activity
D   A cost which is fixed for a certain level of activity and then increases

157 Which of the following would not be illustrated by the cost curve shown below?

A Direct material cost per unit
B Direct labour cost per unit
C Fixed production cost per unit
D Variable production cost per unit

158 Which of the following costs would be most likely to be illustrated by the cost curve given below?

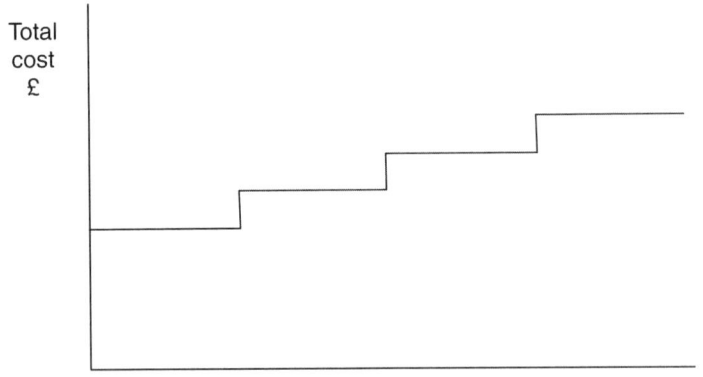

A Sales persons' salaries
B Direct factory labour cost
C Total variable production costs
D Managing director's salary

159 Which of the following costs would be most likely to be illustrated by the cost curve given below?

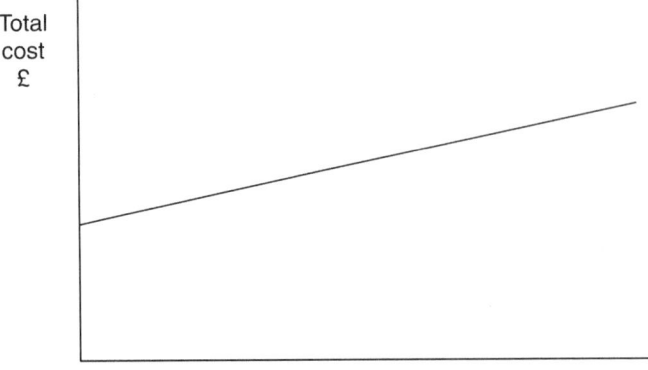

A   Factory rent
B   Heat and power costs
C   Materials cost
D   Factory supervisors' salaries

Data for questions 160 and 161

A factory employs 32 direct production workers and 8 indirect staff. The normal working week is 40 hours and all staff are paid at the basic rate of $6 per hour with overtime hours being paid at a rate of time and a half. During a week all of the employees worked for 43 hours in order to meet general production requirements.

160   What is the direct labour charge for the week?

     A $258
     B $7,680
     C $7,707
     D $8,256

161   What is the indirect labour charge for the week?

     A $1,920
     B $2,064
     C $2,136
     D $2,424

Data for questions 162, 163 and 164

A product that a company manufactures requires 3 kg of material A costing $6.20 per kg and 4 kg of material B costing $5.60 per kg. The product requires 2 hours of labour at a cost of $7.40 per hour. The product is sold in packs of 10 and the packaging for 10 units costs $22. Fixed production costs are $60,000 per annum and selling, distribution and administration costs are $24,000 per annum. The company makes 15,000 units of the product each year.

162   What is the prime cost of the product?

     A $55.80
     B $58.00
     C $62.00
     D $77.80

163   What is the production cost of the product?

     A $55.80
     B $58.00
     C $62.00
     D $77.80

164   What is the total cost of the product?

     A $62.00
     B $63.60
     C $81.80
     D $83.40

165 Which of the following costs would not be included as part of the prime cost of a product?

    A   Hire charge for specialised machine required for product
    B   Rent and rates for factory
    C   Material input for product
    D   Labour cost of product

166 Which costs would not be included as a production cost in marginal costing?

    A   Direct materials costs
    B   Direct labour costs
    C   Variable production costs
    D   Fixed production costs

167 The following statements relate to absorption and marginal costing.

    1   As stock (inventory) levels rise marginal costing profit will be higher than absorption costing profit
    2   Fixed production costs are treated as period costs under marginal costing

Which one of the following is true regarding these statements?

    A   Both statements are incorrect
    B   Both statements are correct
    C   Statement 1 is correct but statement 2 is incorrect
    D   Statement 2 is correct but statement 1 is incorrect

Data for questions 168 and 169

A manufacturing company makes one product which uses 2 kg of raw material at a cost of $3.80 per kg. The product requires 2.5 hours of labour which is paid at $7.80 per hour. The company incurs production costs of $6,000 per month and the factory produces 2,000 units of the product each month. There are no stocks (inventory) of the product at 1 June 20X3 but only 1,600 units of the product were sold in June.

168 What is the closing stock (inventory) valuation at 30 June 20X3 under absorption costing?

    A $10,840
    B $12,040
    C $12,340
    D $48,160

169 What is the closing stock (inventory) valuation at 30 June 20X3 under marginal costing?

    A $10,840
    B $12,040
    C $43,360
    D $54,200

Do you know? – Materials, labour costs and overhead costs

Check that you can fill in the blanks in the statements below before you attempt any questions. If in doubt, you should go back to your BPP Interactive Text and revise first.

- When goods are required by a business the person requiring the goods must normally complete a .... form which must be authorised by an appropriate manager.

- The supplier will then provide a quotation and the purchasing department will then send a .... to the supplier.

- The goods sent will usually be accompanied by a .... note and when the business receives the goods, a .... note will be completed. The supplier will later send a .... to the supplier detailing the amounts due.

- The physical quantity of stock (inventory) is often recorded on a ...... card in the stores department. A similar document known as the .... will be kept by the accounts department.

- Materials issued to production must be classified as either .... or .... materials.

- Hours worked are often recorded on ...., ... or time sheets. Where employees are paid according to the number of units of good production, this is known as a .... system.

- Employers must deduct the following from gross pay before paying net pay to employees.

    – ....
    – ....

- Overheads are made up of the following.

    – ....
    – ....
    – ....

- The first stage of absorption costing is the .... of specific overheads to specific cost centres – then joint overheads are .... to each cost centre on an appropriate basis. The overheads of the .... cost centres must then be reapportioned to the production cost centres on an appropriate basis.

- Once all of the overheads have been apportioned to the production cost centres a(n) .... is determined normally based upon direct labour hours or machine hours.

TRY QUESTIONS 170 TO 214

- *Possible pitfalls. Write down examples of mistakes you should avoid.*

    –
    –
    –
    –

Did you know? – Materials, labour costs and overhead costs

Could you fill in the blanks? The answers are in bold. Use this page for revision purposes as you approach the exam.

- When goods are required by a business the person requiring the goods must normally complete a **purchase requisition** form which must be authorised by an appropriate manager.

- The supplier will then provide a quotation and the purchasing department will then send a **purchase order** to the supplier.

- The goods sent will usually be accompanied by a **delivery** note and when the business receives the goods, a **goods received** note will be completed. The supplier will later send a **purchase invoice** to the supplier detailing the amounts due.

- The physical quantity of stock (inventory) is often recorded on a **bin** card in the stores department. A similar document known as the **stores ledger account** will be kept by the accounts department.

- Materials issued to production must be classified as either **direct** or **indirect** materials.

- Hours worked are often recorded on **clock cards**, **job cards** or time sheets. Where employees are paid according to the number of units of good production, this is known as a **piecework** system.

- Employers must deduct the following from gross pay before paying net pay to employees.

  - **PAYE** (income tax)
  - **Employee's National Insurance Contributions**

- Overheads are made up of the following.

  - **Indirect materials**
  - **Indirect labour**
  - **Indirect expenses**

- The first stage of absorption costing is the **allocation** of specific overheads to specific cost centres – then joint overheads are **apportioned** to each cost centre on an appropriate basis. The overheads of the **service** cost centres must then be reapportioned to the production cost centres on an appropriate basis.

- Once all of the overheads have been apportioned to the production cost centres a(n) **overhead absorption rate** is determined normally based upon direct labour hours or machine hours.

TRY QUESTIONS 170 TO 214

- *Possible pitfalls.*

  - **Not understanding the importance of correct coding**
  - **Not being able to describe the material control cycle**
  - **Not being able to analyse gross earnings**
  - **Not being able to apportion and absorb indirect costs**

Objective test questions 170–214: Materials, labour costs and overhead costs

170 An organisation uses a coding system which identifies each individual supplier by using the first three letters of their name followed by three digits.

Which of the following will appear first when the suppliers are listed in descending order?

A   SLI003
B   SHO006
C   SHE002
D   SKI010

171 Consider the following statements.

1   When costs are coded it is the VAT inclusive amount that must be coded
2   An alphanumeric code is one in which both letters and numbers appear

Which one of the following is correct with regard to the above statements?

A   Both statements are correct
B   Both statements are incorrect
C   Statement 1 is correct but statement 2 is incorrect
D   Statement 1 is incorrect but statement 2 is correct

172 The fixed assets of a business are coded within the numerical range of 3000 to 3050. The third digit in the code represents the type of fixed asset as follows.

1   Land and buildings
2   Plant and machinery
3   Motor vehicles
4   Fixtures and fittings
5   Office equipment

The final digit in the code represents the department of the organisation where the fixed asset is used as follows.

1   Factory
2   Stores
3   Warehouse
4   Accounts
5   General administration

What would be the code given to the purchases of a new desk for the chief accountant?

A   3045
B   3054
C   3044
D   3055

173 Which of the following documents in the purchases cycle would be generated by the supplier?

A   Purchase order
B   Credit note
C   Purchase requisition
D   Goods received note

174 Which of the following documents in the purchases cycle would be generated by the purchaser?

    A   Delivery note
    B   Invoice
    C   Purchase requisition
    D   Credit note

175 Which of the following would not appear as an addition or deduction on the face of a purchase invoice received from a supplier?

    A   Cash discount
    B   Trade discount
    C   Net cost of goods
    D   VAT (sales tax)

176 Goods have been purchased with a list price of $1,000. A 10% trade discount has been given and a 2% cash discount. The goods are standard rated at 17.5% for VAT (sales tax).

How much VAT (sales tax) would appear on the invoice?

    A $154.35
    B $157.50
    C $171.85
    D $175.00

177 Which one of the following is the correct sequential flow of documents in the purchase of goods on credit?

    A   Purchase order, purchase requisition, goods received note, delivery note, invoice
    B   Purchase requisition, purchase order, goods received note, delivery note, invoice
    C   Purchase requisition, purchase order, delivery note, goods received note, invoice
    D   Purchase order, purchase requisition, invoice, delivery note, goods received note

178 When a purchase invoice is received from a supplier which documents should it be checked to?

    A   Purchase requisition and delivery note
    B   Purchase order and goods received note
    C   Advice note and delivery note
    D   Purchase requisition and goods received note

179 Which of the following defines free stock (inventory)?

    A   Stock (inventory) on hand + stock (inventory) on order – stock (inventory) scheduled for use
    B   Stock (inventory) on hand – stock (inventory) on order – stock (inventory) scheduled for use
    C   Stock (inventory) on hand + stock (inventory) on order + stock (inventory) scheduled for use
    D   Stock (inventory) on hand – stock (inventory) on order + stock (inventory) scheduled for use

180 A business buys and sells a finished product. At 1 March 20X3 there are 120 units of this product in stock. The estimated sales over the next three months of this product are:

March	500 units
April	600 units
May	540 units

The stores manager wishes there to be 150 units in stock at the end of May.
How many units of this product should be ordered now?

    A   1,370 units
    B   1,610 units
    C   1,640 units
    D   1,670 units

181   During week 14 a manufacturing business issued $19,600 of direct materials to the factory and $3,200 of indirect materials.

What is the double entry for these issues of materials?

A	Debit	Materials control	$22,800	
	Credit	Work in progress		$19,600
	Credit	Production overhead control		$3,200
B	Debit	Work in progress	$19,600	
	Debit	Production overhead control	$3,200	
	Credit	Materials control		$22,800
C	Debit	Work in progress	$3,200	
	Debit	Production overhead control	$19,600	
	Credit	Materials control		$22,800
D	Debit	Materials control	$22,800	
	Credit	Work in progress		$3,200
	Credit	Production overhead control		$19,600

182   Consider the following statements.

1   A bin card records the quantity of stock (inventory) on hand whereas a store ledger account records the monetary value of the stock (inventory) on hand

2   A perpetual inventory system is one where each receipt or issue of material is recorded as it takes place

Which one of the following is correct with regard to the above statements?

A   Both statements are correct
B   Both statements are incorrect
C   Statement 1 is correct but statement 2 is incorrect
D   Statement 1 is incorrect but statement 2 is correct

183   When materials are purchased on credit and an interlocking costing system is in use what is the double entry for the purchase?

A	Debit	Materials control
	Credit	Creditors (payables)
B	Debit	Materials control
	Credit	Cost ledger control
C	Debit	Creditors
	Credit	Materials control
D	Debit	Cost ledger control
	Credit	Materials control

184   Which member of staff is most likely to raise a materials requisition?

A   Stores manager
B   Cost accountant
C   Purchasing manager
D   Production manager

185 An employee is paid on a piecework basis as follows.

Up to 100 units per week $2.40 per unit
101 to 120 units per week $2.70 per unit
121 units or more per week $3.00 per unit

Only the additional units qualify for the higher rate and rejected units do not qualify for payment.

In a week when the employee produced 133 units of which 11 were rejected what would be the employee's gross pay for the week?

A $297
B $300
C $333
D $366

186 A manufacturing organisation has 24 employees who are paid a basic hourly rate of $6.00 for a standard 38 hour week with any overtime hours being paid at a rate of time and a half. In a typical week the employees all work 4 hours of overtime and produce 2,500 units of the organisation's product.

What is the total unit labour cost for the product?

A $2.19
B $2.30
C $2.42
D $2.53

187 A manufacturing organisation operates a piecework system of wage payment whereby each employee is paid $7.40 per unit for the first 25 units produced in a week and $8.20 per unit for any units in excess of this amount. There are 33 employees and it is expected that each will produce 29 units per week.

What is the total unit labour cost?

A $6.60
B $7.40
C $7.51
D $8.20

188 A manufacturing organisation employs 100 factory workers who are all paid at an hourly rate of $7.00 for a 38 hour week. Any overtime hours are paid at time and a half. On average each unit of the product the factory makes takes 4 hours and in an average week each employee works 4 hours of overtime.

The management has recently installed new machinery which it is estimated should reduce the time taken to produce one unit of the product to 3.5 hours. The employees will continue to work the same amount of overtime.

What will be the increase in the number of units made each week now the machinery has been installed?

A 35 units
B 135 units
C 150 units
D 250 units

Data for questions 189 and 190

An employee is paid an hourly rate of $6.80 for a 40 hour week with overtime paid at a rate of time and a half. In one week the employee worked for 45 hours.

The PAYE (income tax) to be deducted for the week is $58, the employees' National Insurance Contribution is $31 and the employer's National Insurance Contribution is $34.

189 What is the employee's net pay for the week?

    A $183
    B $200
    C $234
    D $323

190 An employee is paid an hourly rate of $6.80 for a 40 hour week with overtime paid at a rate of time and a half. In one week the employee worked for 45 hours.

The PAYE (income tax) to be deducted for the week is $58, the employees' National Insurance Contribution is $31 and the employer's National Insurance Contribution is $34.

What is the wages cost to the employer for this employee's work for the week?

    A $268
    B $306
    C $323
    D $357

Data for questions 191 and 192

These are all elements of payroll costs.

1 Gross pay
2 PAYE (income tax)
3 Employer's NIC
4 Employee's NIC

191 Which of the above affect the employee's net pay?

    A   1, 2 and 4
    B   1, 2 and 3
    C   1 and 2 only
    D   1,2, 3 and 4

192 Which of the above costs are costs to the employer?

    A   1 and 3 only
    B   1 and 4 only
    C   2, 3 and 4
    D   1, 2, 3 and 4

193 Consider the following statements.

1 Overtime payments are generally treated as indirect costs
2 The cost of idle time is generally treated as an indirect cost

Which one of the following is correct regarding the above statements?

    A   Both statements are correct
    B   Both statements are incorrect
    C   Statement 1 is correct but statement 2 is incorrect
    D   Statement 1 is incorrect but statement 2 is correct

Data for questions 194 and 195

During the month of September 20X3 the following labour hours were worked.

Direct production workers – 2,300 hours plus 500 hours of overtime

Indirect workers – 640 hours including 120 hours of overtime

The direct workers are paid $7.20 per hour and the indirect workers $6.20 per hour. Overtime hours are paid at time and a half. Of the hours paid to the direct production workers 100 of these were idle time hours.

194   What is the direct labour cost for the month?

    A $16,560
    B $16,740
    C $19,440
    D $20,160

195   What is the indirect labour cost for the month?

    A $3,224
    B $4,340
    C $6,140
    D $6,860

196   At the end of week 23 a business made a payment for net wages of $17,800. This was after deductions for PAYE and NIC of $5,900. Of the gross amount of $23,700, $3,700 was for indirect wages and the remainder was for direct workers' wages.

What is the double entry for the labour costs for the week?

A	Debit	Wages control	$23,700	
	Credit	Work in progress		$20,000
	Credit	Production overhead		$3,700
B	Debit	Wages control	$23,700	
	Credit	Work in progress		$3,700
	Credit	Production overhead		$20,000
C	Debit	Work in progress	$20,000	
	Debit	Production overhead	$3,700	
	Credit	Wages control		$23,700
D	Debit	Work in progress	$3,700	
	Debit	Production overhead	$20,000	
	Credit	Wages control		$23,700

197   During the month of July 20X3 the gross pay of the direct production workers in a manufacturing business was $32,000 with deductions for PAYE (income tax) and national insurance contribution of $10,600. Three quarters of the wages bill is for direct production workers.

What is the amount to be debited to the work in progress account?

    A $5,350
    B $8,000
    C $16,050
    D $24,000

Data for questions 198 and 199

In week 23 the direct production workers of an organisation worked for 740 hours including 110 hours of overtime. The indirect workers worked for 200 hours which included 40 hours of overtime. Included in the direct workers' hours were 50 hours of idle time. The direct production workers have a basic rate of $8.40 per hour and the indirect workers have a basic rate of $6 per hour. All overtime is paid at time plus one third.

198   What is the amount to be debited to the work in progress account?

    A $2,008
    B $5,796
    C $6,216
    D $6,524

199   What is the amount to be debited to the production overhead control account?

    A $1,280
    B $1,588
    C $2,008
    D $5,796

Data for questions 200 and 201

During week 23 a business incurred gross wages of $33,420. There were deductions for PAYE (income tax) of $5,680 and employee's National Insurance Contributions of $3,160. The employer's National Insurance Contribution for the week was $3,870.

200   What is the amount of cash that the employer will pay as net wages?

    A $20,710
    B $24,580
    C $27,740
    D $33,420

201   What is the wage cost to the employer for the week?

    A $29,550
    B $33,420
    C $37,290
    D $40,450

202   What is the term that is used to describe the process of charging an entire expense to a single cost centre?

    A   Allocation
    B   Apportionment
    C   Absorption
    D   Re-apportionment

203   What is the term used to describe the process of sharing an expense amongst a number of cost centres?

    A   Allocation
    B   Apportionment
    C   Absorption
    D   Re-apportionment

204 A factory has two production cost centres, assembly and finishing, as well as two service cost centres, maintenance and stores. The rent and rates for the next period is anticipated to be $40,000. The floor area occupied by each of the cost centres is:

Assembly   2,000 m²
Finishing   1,400 m²
Stores   1,000 m²
Maintenance   600 m²

What amount should be apportioned to the stores cost centre for rent and rates?

A   Nil
B $8,000
C $11,200
D $16,000

---

205 In a factory the stores cost centre overheads are to be reapportioned to the three production cost centres. What is the most appropriate basis for reapportionment?

A   Number of employees per production cost centre
B   Value of machinery in each production cost centre
C   Number of materials requisitions by each cost centre
D   Machine hours in each cost centre

---

206 A factory has two production cost centres, assembly and finishing, as well as two service cost centres, maintenance and stores. After the allocation and apportionment of overheads the following totals have been established:

	Assembly $	Finishing $	Maintenance $	Stores $
Allocated and apportioned overheads	52,400	41,300	18,590	15,200

The maintenance department is estimated to spend 400 hours in the assembly cost centre and 250 hours in the finishing cost centre. The assembly cost centre will make 140 materials requisitions during the next period but the finishing cost centre will only make 60 materials requisitions.

What is the total production overhead for the assembly department?

A $22,080
B $52,400
C $53,010
D $74,480

---

207 A factory has two production cost centres, A and B, and two service cost centres, stores and the canteen. The overheads for each cost centre after allocation and apportionment are as follows.

	Production cost centres		Service cost centres	
	A $	B $	Stores $	Canteen $
Allocated and apportioned overhead	44,210	38,760	16,280	21,150

You are also given the following information about the cost centres.

	A	B
Number of employees	40	50
Number of materials requisitions	200	240

What is the total amount of service cost centre cost to be reapportioned to production cost centre B?

A $20,580
B $20,630
C $59,340
D $59,390

Data for questions 208 and 209

You are given the following details about the two production cost centres of a business.

	Manufacturing	Finishing
Budgeted overhead	$245,600	$185,400
Labour hours	38,000	88,000
Machine hours	80,000	20,000

The manufacturing cost centre is a largely machine based department whereas the finishing cost centre is very much labour based.

208 What is the overhead absorption rate in the manufacturing cost centre per machine hour (to the nearest cent)?

    A $2.11
    B $3.07
    C $6.46
    D $9.27

209 What is the overhead absorption rate per labour hour in the finishing cost centre (to the nearest cent)?

    A $2.11
    B $3.07
    C $6.46
    D $9.27

210 One of the products that a factory makes spends 3 machine hours in the assembly department and 2 labour hours in the packaging department. The overhead absorption rates for each department are as follows.

Assembly $2.66 per machine hour
Packaging $1.75 per labour hour

What is the total amount of overhead to be absorbed into the cost of the product?

    A $4.41
    B $8.82
    C $10.57
    D $11.48

211 A factory produces a product called the ZZ which has direct materials costs per unit of $4.20 and a direct labour cost per unit of $4.65. Each unit of the ZZ spends half an hour in the assembly department and quarter of an hour being packaged. The overhead absorption rates are $4.80 per hour in the assembly department and $3.60 per hour in the packaging department.

What is the total production cost of one unit of the ZZ?

    A $3.30
    B $8.40
    C $8.85
    D $12.15

212 Consider the following statements.

    1   All expenses are overheads
    2   Service cost centre overheads should be apportioned to production cost centres

Which one of the following is correct with regard to the above statements?

A   Both are correct

B   Both are incorrect

C   Statement 1 is correct but statement 2 is incorrect

D   Statement 1 is incorrect but statement 2 is correct

---

213   A business has two production departments, manufacturing and finishing. Details of these production departments are given below.

	Manufacturing	Finishing
Budgeted overhead	$58,900	$36,500
Budgeted labour hours	10,000	12,000
Budgeted machine hours	40,000	3,000

Overheads in the manufacturing department are absorbed on the basis of machine hours and in the finishing department on the basis of labour hours.

One product, the Gant, has the following details.

	Manufacturing	Finishing
Labour hours per unit	4	2
Machine hours per unit	6	1

How much total overhead would be included in the cost of one unit of the Gant (to the nearest cent)?

A $8.92

B $11.90

C $11.96

D $14.90

---

214   A factory has two production departments, assembly and packaging. One of the products made in the factory is the Edd. Details of the departments and the Edd are given below.

	Assembly	Packaging
Budgeted overhead	$104,300	$64,500
Budgeted machine hours	50,000	10,000
Budgeted labour hours	25,000	30,000
Edd – labour hours per unit	4	3
Edd – machine hours per unit	7	1

Overheads are absorbed on the machine hour basis in the assembly department and on the labour hour basis in the packaging department.

What is the total production overhead to be absorbed into each unit of the Edd (to the nearest cent)?

A $10.51

B $14.81

C $16.78

D $21.08

Do you know? – Information for comparison, variances, marginal costing and decision making

Check that you can fill in the blanks in the statements below before you attempt any questions. If in doubt, you should go back to your BPP Interactive Text and revise first.

- Information for comparison may be .... or ....

- If the actual level of production is different from the original budget, then .... budgets should be used for comparison.

- Budget comparisons are popular because they show whether budget holders are achieving their ....

- .... help budget holders to perform their function of control. The reports are especially useful if they separate controllable from non-controllable variances.

- .... highlights variances which might need investigating.

- Variances can be interdependent.

- The three revenue variances are the .... variance, the .... variance and the .... variance.

- The three cost variances are the .... variance, the .... variance and the ..../......... .... variance.

- Revenue variances result from a difference in .... or a difference in ....

- Cost variances result from a difference in .... or a difference in ..../......... with which resources are used.

- Assessing the contribution which units sold make towards fixed costs is a useful technique known as ....

- Contribution per unit of a .... should be used to decide between products if there is a constraint on production.

- The margin of safety gives a measure of the degree to which sales have to fall before the .... is reached.

- CVP analysis does have limitations. It is only valid within a .... of output volumes. It measures profitability but does not consider the volume of capital employed to achieve such profits.

TRY QUESTIONS 215 TO 247

- *Possible pitfalls. Write down examples of mistakes you should avoid.*

    –

    –

    –

    –

Did you know? – Information for comparison, variances, marginal costing and decision making

Could you fill in the blanks? The answers are in bold. Use this page for revision purposes as you approach the exam.

- Information for comparison may be **financial** or **non-financial**.

- If the actual level of production is different from the original budget, then **flexible** budgets should be used for comparison.

- Budget comparisons are popular because they show whether budget holders are achieving their **targets**.

- **Variance reports** help budget holders to perform their function of control. The reports are especially useful if they separate controllable from non-controllable variances.

- **Exception reporting** highlights variances which might need investigating.

- Variances can be interdependent.

- The three revenue variances are the **total sales revenue** variance, the **activity** variance and the **selling price** variance.

- The three cost variances are the **total direct cost** variance, the **activity** variance and the **purchase price/efficiency of usage** variance.

- Revenue variances result in a difference in **quantity sold** or a difference in **selling price**.

- Cost variances result from a difference in **quantity produced** or a difference in **price paid/efficiency** with which resources are used.

- Assessing the contribution which units sold make towards fixed costs is a useful technique known as **marginal costing**.

- Contribution per unit of a **limiting factor** should be used to decide between products if there is a constraint on production.

- The margin of safety gives a measure of the degree to which sales have to fall before the **breakeven point** is reached.

- CVP analysis does have limitations. It is only valid within a **relevant range** of output volumes. It measures profitability but does not consider the volume of capital employed to achieve such profits.

TRY QUESTIONS 215 TO 247

- *Possible pitfalls include the following (you may have thought of others)*
    - **Not understanding the concept of flexible budgets**
    - **Not being able to identify whether variances are favourable or adverse**
    - **Not being able to identify possible causes of variances**
    - **Not being able to calculate contribution, breakeven point and margin of safety**

Objective test questions 215–247: Information for comparison, variances, marginal costing and decision making

215 Which of the following terms defines a flexible budget?

A   A budget that is added to as each month passes
B   A budget that has not yet been agreed
C   A budget that reflects the actual activity level
D   A budget that is in the process of being altered

216 A business has set its production budget on the basis of production of 15,000 units of its single product. The direct materials budget totals $100,500. In fact production was only 14,600 units during the period.

What is the flexed budget total for direct materials (to the nearest $)?

A $97,820
B $100,100
C $100,500
D $103,253

217 A business's budgeted labour cost is $84,600 for the month of June 20X3. However production in June was 1,400 more than the budgeted production level of 12,500 units.

What is the flexed budget total for direct labour (to the nearest $)?

A $75,124
B $76,079
C $94,075
D $95,270

218 Which of the following provide meaningful comparisons for the person receiving the information?

1   Restaurant takings on Friday night compared to Monday night reported to the owner

2   Daily production output for the last week on an automated production line for the production manager

3   Quarterly sales compared to those of the same quarter in the previous year reported to the sales director

A   1 and 2 only
B   1 and 3 only
C   2 and 3 only
D   All three

219 Consider the following statements.

1   Favourable variances are always good for an organisation
2   Variance reporting is the comparison of the actual results with the original budget

Which one of the following is correct with regard to the statements above?

A   Both statements are correct
B   Both statements are incorrect
C   Statement 1 is correct but statement 2 is incorrect
D   Statement 1 is incorrect but statement 2 is correct

220 The budgeted direct materials cost for a product was $12.30 per unit. During the month of June production details were as follows.

Budget   5,000 units
Actual   5,300 units

The total materials cost for the month was $60,000.

What was the direct materials variance comparing actual with the flexed budget?

A $1,500 adverse
B $1,500 favourable
C $5,190 adverse
D $5,190 favourable

221 A business has budgeted to produce 32,000 units of its product during the first quarter of the year but in fact production was 35,000 units. The budgeted direct materials cost is $3.20 per unit. The actual cost of the materials for the quarter was $110,000.

What was the direct materials variance comparing actual with the flexed budget?

A $2,000 adverse
B $2,000 favourable
C $7,600 adverse
D $7,600 favourable

222 The budgeted direct labour cost for a product was $6.80 per unit. During the month of September production details were as follows.

Budget   12,000 units

The total labour cost for the month was $85,200.

What was the total direct labour variance comparing actual with the fixed budget?

A $1,840 adverse
B $1,840 favourable
C $3,600 adverse
D $3,600 favourable

223 What is exception reporting?

A   Reporting of exceptional activities within an organisation
B   Reporting only controllable matters to managers
C   Reporting only of variances which exceed a certain amount
D   Reporting of all variances to the relevant manager

224 A business has a budgeted direct materials cost per unit of $6.00. During the month of October production details were as follows.

Budget   3,400 units
Actual   3,700 units

The actual materials cost for the month was $25,600.

What was the direct materials variance as a percentage of the budgeted figure, comparing actual with the flexed budget?

A   15.3% adverse
B   15.3% favourable
C   25.5% adverse
D   25.5% favourable

225 A business has a budgeted direct labour cost per unit of $15.50. During the month of December production details were as follows.

Budget   12,600 units

The actual labour cost for the month was $199,400.

What was the total direct labour variance as a percentage of the budgeted figure, comparing actual with the fixed budget?

A   2.1% adverse
B   2.1% favourable
C   7.2% adverse
D   7.2% favourable

226 Consider the following factors for investigating a variance.

1   Controllability of variance
2   Cost of investigation
3   Personnel involved
4   Trend of variance

Which of these would be a factor that would affect a decision as to whether to investigate the variance?

A   2 and 4 only
B   2, 3 and 4 only
C   1, 2 and 3 only
D   1, 2 and 4 only

227 Given below is a summary of a performance report showing the actual results for a month compared to the flexed budget figures. It is the company's policy that any variance which exceeds 10% of the budgeted figure should be reported and investigated.

	Actual	Flexed budget
	$	$
Direct materials	26,589	24,000
Direct labour	18,337	16,200
Direct expenses	2,172	2,100

Which variances should be investigated?

A   Materials and labour
B   Materials and expenses
C   Labour and expenses
D   All three

Data for questions 228 and 230

A company sells a single product. The sales budget for a period was 8,000 units at a selling price of $2.50 per unit. 8,320 units were actually sold in the period for a total revenue of $19,968.

228 What is the total sales revenue variance?

A $32 Favourable
B $832 Adverse
C $32 Adverse
D $832 Favourable

229   What is the activity variance comparing the fixed budget with the flexible budget?

   A $832 Adverse
   B $800 Favourable
   C $800 Adverse
   D $32 Favourable

230   What is the sales revenue variance comparing actual with the flexed budget?

   A $832 Adverse
   B $602 Favourable
   C $832 Favourable
   D $32 Adverse

Data for questions 231 and 233

Budgeted and actual production of a product X for a period was:

Budget   60,000 units
Actual   62,400 units

The budgeted direct materials cost of the product was $3.20 per unit and a total of $187,200 was incurred on direct materials in the period.

231   What is the total direct cost variance?

   A $4,800 Favourable
   B $12,480 Favourable
   C $4,800 Adverse
   D $12,480 Adverse

232   What is the activity variance comparing the fixed budget with the flexible budget?

   A $6,000 Favourable
   B $7,680 Adverse
   C $12,480 Adverse
   D $4,800 Favourable

233   What is the direct materials variance comparing actual with the flexed budget?

   A $4,800 Favourable
   B $6,000 Adverse
   C $12,480 Favourable
   D $12,480 Adverse

234   What is total contribution?

   A   Revenue less total costs
   B   Revenue less fixed costs
   C   Revenue less variable costs
   D   Revenue less production costs

235 In a situation where a resource is limited what figure is used to determine the optimal production plan?

 A Contribution per unit
 B Profit per unit
 C Contribution per unit of limiting resource
 D Profit per unit of limiting resource

Data for questions 236 and 237

A business makes two products with the following details.

	Product A	Product B
Selling price	$34.00	$16.00
Direct materials $2.00 per kg	16.00	6.00
Direct labour $4 per hour	8.00	4.00
Variable costs	2.00	1.00
Total variable costs	26.00	11.00
Maximum sales quantity	1,000.00	2,000.00

In the next period the amount of materials available is limited to 10,000 kg.

236 How many units of product A should be made if profit is to be maximised?

 A 500 units
 B 800 units
 C 900 units
 D 1,000 units

237 If the optimal production plan is chosen what is the total contribution?

 A $4,000
 B $8,000
 C $10,000
 D $14,000

Data for questions 238 and 239

A business makes a single product and sells it for $34.00 per unit. The budgeted cost of this product is as follows.

	$
Direct materials	10.00
Direct labour	12.00
Variable overhead	6.00
Fixed overhead	2.00
	30.00

It has been budgeted to make 10,000 units of this product.

238 What is the breakeven point in number of units?

 A 1,667 units
 B 3,333 units
 C 5,000 units
 D 10,000 units

239 How many units of this product must be sold in order to make a profit of $50,000?

A   5,833 units
B   8,333 units
C   11,667 units
D   17,500 units

240 A business sells a single product and the details of this product are given below.

	$
Selling price	10.00
Direct materials	3.20
Direct labour	3.60
Variable overhead	1.20
Fixed overhead	0.80
	8.80

What is the contribution to sales ratio?

A   0.12
B   0.20
C   0.32
D   0.48

Data for questions 241 and 242

A business sells a single product and it has budgeted to manufacture and sell 5,000 units in the next year. The selling price of the product is $50 per unit. The costs of the product are as follows.

	$
Direct materials	15.00
Direct labour	14.00
Variable overhead	6.00
Fixed overhead	8.00
	43.00

241 What is the breakeven sales revenue?

A $95,238
B $133,333
C $166,667
D $285,714

242 What sales revenue is required in order to earn a profit of $30,000?

A $100,000
B $166,667
C $233,333
D $500,000

243 The following information is available about the sales of a business's single product.

Sales revenue $108,000 (@ $15 each)
Variable costs $48,600
Fixed costs $35,200

What level of sales is required to break even?

A   5,215 units
B   7,200 units
C $64,000
D $78,225

244 A business sells a single product with the following details.

	$
Selling price	22.00
Direct materials	7.90
Direct labour	5.20
Variable overhead	1.30
Fixed overhead	4.00
	18.40

The business has budgeted to produce and sell 100,000 units.

What is the margin of safety in units?

A   44,944 units
B   47,368 units
C   52,632 units
D   55,056 units

245 A business is budgeting to manufacture and sell 40,000 units of its single product at a price of $68.00 per unit. The direct materials cost is $31.00 per unit, direct labour $24.00 per unit and variable overheads $8.00 per unit. The expected fixed costs are $140,000.

What is the margin of safety as a percentage?

A   27%
B   30%
C   63%
D   70%

246 Given below is a chart.

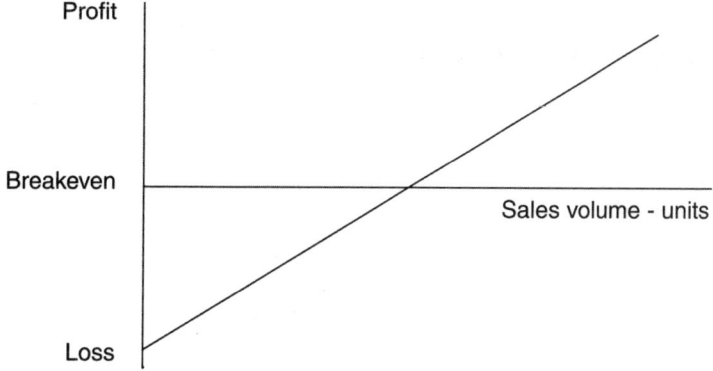

What type of chart is this?

A   Contribution/sales chart

B   Breakeven chart

C   Margin of safety chart

D   Profit/volume chart

247   A business is expecting to manufacture and sell 100,000 units of its single product and its breakeven point is 70,000 units.

If there is an increase in variable costs this will have which of the following effects?

A   Increase in breakeven point and decrease in margin of safety

B   Increase in breakeven point and increase in margin of safety

C   Decrease in breakeven point and increase in margin of safety

D   Decrease in breakeven point and decrease in margin of safety

Answers

Answers to objective test questions 1 – 38: Computer hardware and software

1   C   CD-ROM standards for compact disk read-only memory.

2   D   Peripherals are pieces of IT hardware other than actual computers.

3   B   Dell produce PCs.

4   C   Microsoft Word is wordprocessing software.

5   B   The keyboard is an input device. The screen and the printer are output devices, while the CPU performs the processing function.

6   D   Windows XP is software – an operating system.

7   B   PCs are now widespread throughout organisations.

8   D   A printer need not be connected to the PC – it would still work, displaying its output on the screen. Input devices, such as a keyboard, are necessary, as is the screen. The CPU enables the PC to process the input information.

9   A   The CPU is divided into 3 areas, the control unit which receives program instructions, the ALU (arithmetic and logic unit) which performs the calculations allowing the instructions to be carried out, and the memory which holds the instructions in memory while the computer is operating.

10   C   16 KB is $16 \times 1{,}024$. Answer A (1,024) represents 1 Kilobyte, Answer B (8,388,608) is $8 \times 1{,}024$ or 8 Kb. Answer D (17,179,869,184) is $16 \times 1{,}024 \times 1{,}024 \times 1{,}024$ or 16 Gb.

11   C   Hard disks vary in size, but a typical PC hard disk offers 5 Gb – 10 Gb of storage capacity. A DVD can hold approximately 5 Gb, a CD 650 Mb and a floppy disk 1.44 Mb.

12   A   The mouse is an input device, not a storage device.

13   D   People are able to question and interpret the data they are dealing with.

14   D   DOS is an unfriendly text based operating system. DOS was widely used before the advent of Windows.

15   C   WYSIWIG (what you see is what you get) describes the fact that what you see on the screen is an accurate representation of what will be printed. OCR (optical character recognition), OMR (mark sensing and optical mark reading) and MICR (magnetic ink character recognition) are all computer readable methods of conveying data.

16   C   Laser printers print on to individual sheets of paper. They do not use continuous stationery.

17   A   A LAN is linked by direct cables not by the telecommunications network. A WAN is linked by the telecommunications network.

18   D   It is still vital to take regular back-ups. In fact, even more information will now be held on the computer meaning back-ups are vital.

19   B   Many new mice sold today are optical rather than wheeled.

20   D   Shop assistants quite commonly key in/scan something twice, so (ii) is clearly wrong. Statement (iii) is correct in the sense that EPOS allows better forecasting of demand and stock (inventory) movements, and so less safety stock (inventory).

21   C   Programs and data in current use are stored in RAM memory.

22   D   RAM is supplied on chips which can be plugged in and unplugged fairly easily.

23   C   A LAN uses computer cabling. A WAN requires telecommunications links between sites.

24	C	Statement (ii) is nonsense.
25	C	The application currently being used is stored temporarily in the RAM to enable quick and easy access to the program. The other statements are false.
26	D	When 'booting-up' a PC uses information stored in the ROM. The other statements are false.
27	C	This is the job of the operating system.
28	B	PCs can be backed up to tape if a suitable tape unit or tape drive is attached.
29	B	
30	A	
31	B	
32	B	750 MHz means that the processor completes 750 million cycles, or separate instructions, per second.
33	B	A modem converts signals between analogue and digital formats.
34	B	1 MHz is one million cycles per second.
35	A	Cache memory stores a copy of data most recently read.
36	A	Integrated Services Digital Network.
37	C	Magnetic Ink Character Recognition is used on cheques
38	B	

Answers to objective test questions 39 – 80: Computer skills

39	A	Most electronic mail is sent via the Internet. However, there are security issues with the use of public systems which lead some organisations to investment in private e-mail services.
40	B	The operating system controls the operation of the computer.
41	C	There is no point in devising a spreadsheet if you are not prepared to let it work for you, so answers A and B, are not appropriate.
42	C	Answer B adds across the monthly net profit figures. Answer A subtracts the costs listed from fee income in the year-to-date column. Answer D is effectively the same calculation as answer A. Answer C is wrong: Excel requires an '=' sign to show that it is a formula.
43	A	Both formulae in answer A are correct. Both formulae in answer B are incorrect. Formula (1) in answer B, =C4 – D4/D4 can be translated as $21,500 – $22,000/$22,000 which equals $21,500 – 1. Operations in brackets are performed first, so that, in answer A the result of $21,500 – $22,000 is divided by $22,000. As for formula 2, answer B will generate an *error* message as no priority has been given to one of the calculations: either cell C19 divided by cell C4 is first performed, or cell C4 divided by 30 days.
44	C	E-mail is virtually instantaneous – so long as all systems involved are operational.
45	B	Although computer systems may have some automatic checks on data input, no system is able to identify all incorrect data eg '91' may be entered as '19'.
46	D	
47	C	The Internet is not owned by any one body, but by all of the bodies and individuals that use it.
48	D	No computer system knows exactly what you intended so can not make 100% accurate connections.
49	C	The first three statements are correct. Modems are not used in LANs, therefore (iv) is incorrect.
50	B	Microsoft Access is a database application.
51	C	Some packages (eg Word) can assess the user's grammar, but they do not correct it automatically.
52	B	The Internet can be used for ED1 but it is not governed by ED1 standards.
53	C	
54	B	Intel manufactures computer chips.
55	D	Putting a value in the cell, such as 2860, would mean that the cell was not updated to reflect later changes to the spreadsheet.
56	B	In Excel, placing the $ sign in front of a cell reference makes that reference absolute. When you move or copy a formula absolute cell references do not change.
57	A	The correct formula is =D28+D18. Although D18+D28 looks the same, because it has no = sign it is not treated as a formula. Both of the other options count sub totals as well the cost items.
58	B	Formulae, text and numbers can be entered onto a spreadsheet.
59	D	
60	D	
61	A	Microsoft Internet Explorer is not a search engine, it's a web browser.
62	B	HyperText Transfer Protocol.
63	B	Blind Carbon Copy.
64	A	Option A shows the correct formula.

65	C	Option C shows the correct formula.
66	C	The formula would contain the COUNT function.
67	A	The absolute sign, '$', should be used on the row and column reference for the cell B15.
		Also using the '$' with the column references for C column will give the desired result.
68	C	Spelling and grammar checks in software are unlikely to find this error.
69	B	
70	B	The ^ symbol means 'to the power of'.
71	A	ROUNDUP does what it says – rounds up rather than rounding to the nearest number.
72	A	The Back button takes the user back one page.
73	D	You should be familiar with this concept from hands-on use of the Internet.
74	B	
75	B	COUNT is the appropriate function and B6:B25 the range.
76	A	MAX is the appropriate function.
77	D	A sort, based on column G, should be performed.
78	A	Universal Serial Bus – a type of port and connection.
79	C	Microsoft Internet Explorer is the most widely used web browser.
80	D	

Answers to objective test questions 81 – 100: Security, back-ups and legal issues

81	C	Tape streamer is the correct term.
82	D	Encryption involves the replacement of the correct text by cipher. The transformation from a cipher text to the original is called decryption. An authentication code is a coded check, derived from an algorithm, which can reveal whether a message has been tampered with.
83	A	The Data Protection Act aims to protect the privacy of individuals.
84	B	
85	C	
86	C	All systems should include back-up storage and virus detection software. Passwords are needs if information is to be kept confidential.
87	D	Hackers gain unauthorised access to systems from remote locations. To steal computer hardware requires physical access to the premises where the hardware is kept.
88	B	A logic bomb waits for a specific event to occur before executing.
89	A	
90	B	Archiving involves storing 'old' data on an external storage medium.
91	B	These issues are covered under Data Protection legislation.
92	D	Personal Identification Number.
93	A	
94	D	Option C is incorrect as viruses spread most rapidly via e-mail.
95	C	
96	D	Off-site back-ups will be required should the premises be destroyed (even a fire-proof safe on-site may be damaged or destroyed).
97	A	Iris scanning technology and equipment is too expensive to be feasible for most organisations
98	C	This is the only valid statement.
99	B	Norton Anti-virus is one of the main anti-virus packages in use. McAfee is another.
100	D	Most 'computer errors' are in fact due to 'human error'.

Answers to objective test questions 101 – 120: Introduction to management information and reporting management information

101	C	
102	B	The other three items have been processed in some way to provide meaningful information whereas total sales value per product is the basic data for further processing.
103	B	
104	D	
105	C	
106	D	
107	C	Comparison of actual costs with budgeted costs allows management to control the operations of the business.
108	D	The other three are all internally generated.
109	D	Management accounts are not a legal requirement whereas financial accounts are. Management accounts look at past data as well as future data.
110	A	
111	A	
112	A	
113	B	
114	B	Provided that passwords are used and protected, e-mail can be used for confidential information.
115	C	
116	C	
117	B	
118	D	
119	A	
120	D	

Answers to objective test questions 121 – 130: Business organisation and accounting

121	C	
122	C	Employees would be expected to have read the parts of the policy manual relevant to their role in the organisation.
123	C	
124	B	
125	C	
126	A	
127	C	
128	B	An **integrated system** is one where the cost accounting and financial accounting functions are combined in one set of ledger accounts. An **interlocking system** is one where separate ledgers are kept for cost accounting and for financial accounting.
129	C	
130	A	

Answers to objective test questions 131–169: Management responsibility and performance measurement; cost units, cost classification and profit reporting

131　D

132　C　Managers should only be held responsible for directly attributable costs.

133　C

134　D

135　C

136　A

137　A

Cost per unit in May	$\dfrac{\$51{,}068}{150{,}200} =$	$0.34
Cost per unit in June	$\dfrac{\$67{,}821}{183{,}300} =$	$0.37
Increase		$0.03

138　D　$\text{Index} = \dfrac{16.70}{15.00} \times 100 = 111.3$

139　C

Budgeted production	=	10 units × 40 hours × 15 employees
	=	6,000 units
Actual production	=	6,200 units
Index	=	$\dfrac{6{,}200}{6{,}000} \times 100$
	=	103.3

140　D

Gross profit margin	=	$\dfrac{\$150{,}000 + 50{,}000 - 120{,}000}{\$150{,}000 + 50{,}000} \times 100$
	=	40%

141　A

Operating profit	=	$150,000 + 50,000 − 120,000 − 35,000 − 25,000
	=	$20,000
Operating profit margin	=	$\dfrac{\$20{,}000}{\$150{,}000 + 50{,}000} \times 100$
	=	10%

142　B

Sales	=	$240,000 × 100/30
	=	$800,000
Net profit	=	$\dfrac{\$240{,}000 - \$106{,}000}{\$800{,}000} \times 100$
	=	16.75%

143　D

A	2,000 × 1 hour	2,000
B	800 × 1.5 hours	1,200
C	1,400 × 1.75	2,450
		5,650

144　A

145　B　Efficiency ratio $= \dfrac{\text{standard hours produced}}{\text{actual hours worked}} \times 100$

$= \dfrac{10{,}800}{11{,}400} \times 100$

$= 94.7\%$

146　C　Capacity ratio $= \dfrac{\text{Actual hours worked}}{\text{Budgeted hours}} \times 100$

$= \dfrac{11{,}400}{12{,}000} \times 100$

$= 95.0\%$

147　A　Activity ratio $= \dfrac{\text{Standard hours produced}}{\text{Budgeted hours}} \times 100$

$= \dfrac{10{,}800}{12{,}000} \times 100$

$= 90.0\%$

148　C

149　C　Return on investment $= \dfrac{\text{Profit before tax}}{\text{Capital employed}} \times 100$

$= \dfrac{40{,}000}{340{,}000} \times 100$

$= 11.8\%$

150　C　This is a cost centre not a cost unit.

151　B

152　C

153　D

154　B　A fixed cost

155　D

156　D

157　C

158　A　As activity levels increase, more salesmen will be required.

159　B　Heat and power costs will consist of a fixed standing charge and a variable element for the usage.

160　D　Direct labour cost $=$ 43 hours $\times$ \$6 $\times$ 32 direct workers
　　　　　　　　　　　　 $=$ \$8,256

161　D

	$
Indirect labour	2,064
– indirect workers – basic 43 hours × 8 staff × \$6	
– overtime premium 3 hours × 40 staff × \$3	360
	2,424

162 B

	$
Direct material cost A 3 kg × $6.20	18.6
B 4 kg × $5.60	22.40
Direct labour – 2 hours × $7.40	14.80
Packaging costs ($22/10)	2.20
Prime cost	58.00

163 C

	$
Prime cost	58.00
Fixed production overheads ($60,000/15,000)	4.00
Production cost	62.00

164 B

	$
Production cost	62.00
Selling, distribution etc costs ($24,000/15,000)	1.60
Total cost	63.60

165 B

166 D

167 D   As stock (inventory) levels rise absorption costing profit will be higher than marginal costing profit.

168 B   Absorption cost

	$
Direct materials (2 kg × $3.80)	7.60
Direct labour (2.5 hours × $7.80)	19.50
Production costs ($6,000/2,000)	3.00
	30.10
Closing stock (inventory) (400 units × $30.10)	$12,040

169 A   Marginal cost

	$
Direct materials (2 kg × $3.80)	7.60
Direct labour (2.5 hours × $7.80)	19.50
	27.10
Closing stock (inventory) (400 units × $27.10)	$10,840

Answers to objective test questions 170 – 214: Materials, labour costs and overhead costs

170   A

171   D   It is the amount net of VAT (sales tax) that must be coded for costs and revenue.

172   C

173   B

174   C

175   A   The cash or settlement discount is not deducted until payment is made.

176   A

	$
List price	1,000
Less: trade discount (10% × $1,000)	(100)
	900
Less: cash discount (2% × $900)	(18)
	882
VAT (sales tax) ($882 × 17.5%)	$154.35

177   C

178   B

179   A

180   D

	Units
Sales (500 + 600 + 540)	1,640
Less: opening stock (inventory)	(120)
Add: closing stock (inventory)	150
Order quantity	1,670

181   B

182   A

183   B

184   D

185   B

	$
100 units @ $2.40	240.00
20 units @ $2.70	54.00
2 units @ $3	6.00
	300.00

186   D

		$
Basic wage	24 × 38 hours × $6.00	5,472
Overtime	24 × 4 hours × $9.00	864
		6,336
Labour cost per unit ($6,336/2,500)		$2.53

187   C

	$
25 units × $7.40	185.00
4 × $8.20	32.80
	217.80
Unit labour cost $217.80/29	$7.51

188   C   Current number of units $= \dfrac{100 \times 42 \text{ hours}}{4 \text{ hours per unit}}$

= 1,050 units

New number of units $= \dfrac{100 \times 42 \text{ hours}}{3.5 \text{ hours per unit}}$

= 1,200 units

Increase (1,200 – 1,050)   = 150 units

189   C

	$
Gross pay: basic (40 hours × $6.80)	272.00
overtime (5 hours × $6.80 × 1.5)	51.00
	323.00
PAYE	(58.00)
Employee's NIC	(31.00)
Net pay	234.00

190   D

	$
Gross pay: basic (40 hours × $6.80)	272.00
overtime (5 hours × $6.80 × 1.5)	51.00
Gross pay	323.00
Employer's NIC	34.00
	357.00

191   A

192   A

193   D   It is the overtime premium which is treated as an indirect cost not the total payment for the overtime hours.

194   C

	$
Direct production workers basic hours	
(2,300 + 500 – 100) × $7.20	19,440

195   D

		$
Indirect workers:	(640 – 120) × $6.20	3,224
	120 × $6.20 × 1.5	1,116
Direct workers:	overtime premium	
	(500 × (7.20 × 0.5))	1,800
Idle time hours	(100 × $7.20)	720
		6,860

196   C

197   D

198 B

	$
Direct production workers – basic	
(740 – 50) × $8.40	5,796

199 C

			$
Indirect workers:	basic (200 × $6)		1,200
	overtime premium		
	(40 × $6/3)		80
Direct workers:	overtime premium		
	(110 × $8.40/3)		308
Idle time	(50 × $8.40)		420
			2,008

200 B

	$
Gross pay	33,420
PAYE	(5,680)
Employee's NIC	(3,160)
	24,580

201 C

	$
Gross pay	33,420
Employer's NIC	3,870
	37,290

202 A

203 B

204 B Rent and rates = $40,000/5,000 sq m × 1,000 sq m
= $8,000

205 C

206 D

207 B

		$
Stores	$16,280 × 240/440	8,880
Canteen	$21,150 × 50/90	11,750
		20,630

208 B OAR $= \dfrac{\$245,600}{80,000}$
= $3.07 per machine hour

209 A OAR $= \dfrac{\$185,400}{88,000}$
= $2.11

210 D

		$
Assembly	3 × $2.66	7.98
Packaging	2 × $1.75	3.50
		11.48

211 D

		$
Direct materials		4.20
Direct labour		4.65
Assembly	($4.80 × ½)	2.40
Packaging	($3.60 × ¼)	0.90
		12.15

212 D Some expenses may be direct expenses of a product or job. Overheads are indirect expenses.

213 D Manufacturing OAR = $58,900/40,000 = $1.47 per machine hour
Finishing OAR   = $36,500/12,000 = $3.04 per labour hour

Gant		$
Manufacturing	6 × $1.47	8.82
Finishing	2 × $3.04	6.08
		14.90

214 D Assembly OAR = $104,300/50,000 = $2.09 per machine hour
Packaging OAR = $64,500/30,000 = $2.15 per labour hour

Edd		$
Assembly	7 × $2.09	14.63
Packaging	3 × $2.15	6.45
		21.08

Answers to objective test questions 215–247: Information for comparison, variances, marginal costing and decision making

215   C

216   A   Flexed budget   = $100,500 × 14,600/15,000
                          = $97,820

217   C   Flexed budget   = $84,600 ×13,900/12,500
                          = $94,075

218   C   Restaurant takings are likely to be much lower on a Monday night than on a Friday night.

219   B   Favourable variances may not always be good. For example, a favourable materials variance might be achieved by buying poorer quality material which means that the labour force have to spend much longer working on the material leading to an adverse labour variance.

Variance reporting is the reporting of differences between the actual results and the flexed budget not the original budget.

220   D

	$	
Flexed budget 5,300 units × $12.30	65,190	
Actual cost	60,000	
Variance	5,190	favourable

221   B

	$	
Flexed budget 35,000 × $3.20	112,000	
Actual cost	110,000	
Variance	2,000	favourable

222   C

	$	
Should have cost 12,000 units × $6.80	81,600	
Actual cost	85,200	
Variance	3,600	adverse

223   C

224   A

	$	
Flexed budget 3,700 units × $6.00	22,200	
Actual cost	25,600	
Variance	3,400	adverse
Percentage of budget 3,400/22,200 × 100 =	15.3%	adverse

225 A

	$	
12,600 units × $15.50	195,300	
Actual cost	199,400	
Variance	4,100	adverse
Percentage of budget 4,100/195,300 × 100 =	2.1%	adverse

226 D

227 A

Direct materials	2,589/24,000 × 100 =	10.8%
Direct labour	2,137/16,200 × 100 =	13.2%
Direct expenses	72/2,100 × 100 =	3.4%

228 C

	$	
Revenue should have been $2.50 × 8,000	20,000	
Revenue actually was	19,968	
	32	adverse

229 B

Budgeted sales volume	8,000	units
Actual sales volume	8,320	units
Activity variance in units	320	units (favourable)
× Budgeted selling price per unit	× $2.50	
Activity variance	$ 800	favourable

230 A

	$	
Sales revenue from 8,320 units should have been (× $2.50)	20,800	
But was	19,968	
	832	adverse

231 A

	$	
Should have cost $3.20 × 60,000	192,000	
Did cost	187,200	
	4,800	favourable

232 B

Budget production volume	60,000	units
Actual production volume	62,400	units
Activity variance in units	2,400	units A
× budgeted cost per unit	× $3.20	
Activity variance	$7,680	adverse

233 C

	$	
Material cost for 62,400 units should have been (× $3.20)	199,680	
But was	187,200	
Purchase price variance	12,480	favourable

234 C

235 C

236   A

	Product A	Product B
Contribution per unit	$8.00	$5.00
Contribution per kg	$1.00	$1.67
Ranking	2	1

Therefore optimal production plan:

	Units produced	Kgs used	Contribution $
Product B	2,000	6,000	10,000
Product A (bal fig)	500	4,000	4,000
		10,000	14,000

237   D

238   B   Contribution per unit $= \$34 - 10 - 12 - 6 = \$6$

Fixed overheads $= \$2 \times 10{,}000 \text{ units} = \$20{,}000$

Breakeven point $= \dfrac{\$20{,}000}{\$6}$

$= 3{,}333 \text{ units}$

239   C   Number of units $= \dfrac{\$20{,}000 + \$50{,}000}{\$6}$

$= 11{,}667 \text{ units}$

240   B   C/S ratio $= \dfrac{\$(10 - 3.20 - 3.60 - 1.20)}{\$10}$

$= 0.20$

241   B   Contribution per unit $= \$(50 - 15 - 14 - 6) \quad = \$15$

C/S ratio $= \dfrac{\$15}{\$50}$

$= 0.30$

Fixed costs $= 5{,}000 \text{ units} \times \$8.00$
$= \$40{,}000$

Breakeven revenue $= \dfrac{£40{,}000}{0.3}$

$= \$133{,}333$

242   C   Revenue $= \dfrac{\$40{,}000 + \$30{,}000}{0.3}$

$= \$233{,}333$

243   C   Number of units sold $= \$108,000/15$

                                $= 7,200$

	$
Sales	108,000
Variable costs	(48,600)
Contribution	59,400

Contribution per unit $= \$59,400/7,200$

                         $= \$8.25$

Breakeven point in units $= \dfrac{\$35,200}{\$8.25}$

                            $= 4,267$ units

C/S ratio $= \dfrac{\$59,400}{\$108,000}$

             $= 0.55$

Sales revenue $= \dfrac{\$35,200}{0.55}$

                 $= \$64,000$

244   B   Contribution per unit $= \$(22.00 - 7.90 - 5.20 - 1.30) = \$7.60$

                Fixed overheads $= 100,000 \times \$4$ $= \$400,000$

Breakeven point $= \dfrac{\$400,000}{\$7.60}$

                   $= 52,632$ units

Margin of safety $= 100,000 - 52,632$

                    $= 47,368$ units

245   B   Contribution per unit $= \$(68 - 31 - 24 - 8)$ $= \$5$

Breakeven point $= \dfrac{\$140,000}{\$5}$

                   $= 28,000$ units

Margin of safety $= 40,000 - 28,000$

                    $= 12,000$

Margin of safety % $= \dfrac{12,000}{40,000}$

                      $= 30\%$

246   D

247   A

124   BPP
LEARNING MEDIA

Mock exams

CAT

Introductory Paper 2

Information for Management Control

Mock Examination 1

Pilot Paper

Question Paper	
Time allowed	**2 hours**
ALL FIFTY questions are compulsory and MUST be answered	

DO NOT OPEN THIS PAPER UNTIL YOU ARE READY TO START UNDER EXAMINATION CONDITIONS

ALL FIFTY questions are compulsory and must be attempted

Please use the candidate Registration Sheet provided to indicate your chosen answer to each multiple choice question. Each question carries two marks

1   Which of the following is an example of computer hardware?

    A   Compiler
    B   Internal modem
    C   Operating system
    D   Spreadsheet

2   Two statements follow about the purpose of a computer's mouse:

    (1)   The purpose of a mouse is to control the cursor on the computer screen.
    (2)   The purpose of a mouse is to let people play computer games quickly and cheaply.

    Which of the following is correct with regard to the above statements?

    A   Both statements are false
    B   Both statements are true
    C   Statement 1 is false but Statement 2 is true
    D   Statement 1 is true but Statement 2 is false

3   The main piece of computer equipment is called the central processing unit (CPU).

    What is the best definition of a central processing unit?

    A   It contains all the computer programmes
    B   It is created by a computer programmer
    C   It is a programmed computer unit
    D   It is the piece of computer equipment for processing data

4   The date of birth of each employee is held on a computer system.

    Of what is 'date of birth' an example?

    A   A database
    B   A field
    C   A file
    D   A record

5   Which correctly states the maximum amount of data (approximately) that can be stored on the computer storage devices?

    A   3½" floppy 5Gb: CD-ROM 650Mb: DVD 1.44Mb
    B   3½" floppy 1.44Mb: CD-ROM 5Gb: DVD 650Mb
    C   3½" floppy 650Mb: CD-ROM 1.44Mb: DVD 5Gb
    D   3½" floppy 1.44Mb: CD-ROM 650Mb: DVD 5Gb

6   Why is it necessary to switch off your computer before going home at the end of the day?

    A   For confidentiality and security reasons
    B   To reduce fire hazards
    C   For both of the above reasons
    D   For neither of the above reasons

7   What is NOT now a common method of security when using computer databases?

   A   Identify names
   B   Key for the lock on the computer
   C   Passwords
   D   Restrictions on access rights

8   Why are PINs used?

   A   To ensure employees perform their work correctly
   B   To increase the capacity of the computer
   C   To restrict access by unauthorised personnel
   D   None of the above reasons

9   A networked PC system is backed up each evening and the minimum size of the backed-up data is 80Mb.

   What is the most likely back-up medium?

   A   A floppy disk
   B   A high speed printer
   C   A separate part of the file server's hard disk
   D   A zip disk cartridge

10 What term is applied to the practice of retaining computer files no longer required on a daily basis in their original form for storage elsewhere?

   A   Archiving
   B   Microfiching
   C   Microfilming
   D   Shredding

11 You work in your firm's computerised payroll section. Back-ups of confidential and important computer master files containing payroll information need to be securely stored within the office.

   Ideally, where should such files be kept?

   A   Box file on the office shelf
   B   Fire-proof locked cabinet
   C   Locked filing cabinet
   D   Payroll clerk's desktop drawer

12 An employee believes that incorrect information held about himself on his company's human resources system has contributed to him not being promoted. The company has acknowledged that the information was incorrect and has now corrected it. However, the employee is now seeking compensation for the loss of income that he feels this error has caused him over the years.

   Under what legislation could the employee seek such compensation?

   A   Computer Misuse Act
   B   Computer Protection Act
   C   Data Misuse Act
   D   Data Protection Act

13 What is the scientific term for facts, figures and information?

   A   Consultancy
   B   Data
   C   Referencing
   D   Statistics

14   Which one of the following is true with regard to management information?

A   It is the same as operating information
B   It must be produced by a computer
C   It should be completely accurate, regardless of cost
D   It should be produced if its cost is less than the increased revenue it leads to

15   Which one of the following is NOT an attribute of effective communication?

A   Clarity
B   Completeness
C   Complexity
D   Relevance

16   Which one of the following is an example of internal information for the wages department of a large company?

A   A Code of Practice issued by the Institute of Directors
B   A new national minimum wage
C   Changes to tax coding arrangements issued by the Inland Revenue
D   The company's employees' schedule of hours worked

17   Which one of the following would be included in the financial accounts, but may be excluded from the cost accounts?

A   Bank interest and charges
B   Depreciation of storeroom handling equipment
C   Direct material costs
D   Factory manager's salary

18   Which one of the following terms is applied to the systematic arrangement of numerical data in order to provide a logical account of analytical results?

A   Computerisation
B   Pictorialisation
C   Quantification
D   Tabulation

19   The phrase 'Laura bought a loaf of bred' is contained in a word processed document. It contains a mistake because 'bred' should really read 'bread'.

What is the most likely way of the author finding this error?

A   Ask a colleague to carefully proof-read the document and indicate any mistakes
B   Check the document with the grammar checker in the word processing software
C   Check the document with the spell checker in the word processing software
D   Use a document imaging system to identify incorrectly used words

20   When communicating information, which of the following determine(s) the choice of method used?

(1)   Comparative cost
(2)   Degree of confidentiality
(3)   Speed of delivery

A   1 only
B   3 only
C   1 and 2 only
D   1, 2 and 3

21   Two statements follow about the purpose of an e-mail system:

(1)   The purpose of an e-mail system is to send and receive data a computer can work with.
(2)   The purpose of an e-mail system is to send and receive messages quickly and cheaply.

Which one of the following is correct with regard to the above statements?

A   Both statements are false
B   Both statements are true
C   Statement 1 is false and Statement 2 is true
D   Statement 1 is true and Statement 2 is false

22   What is the most appropriate definition of an office?

A   A centre for exchanging information between businesses
B   A centre for information and administration
C   A place where information is stored
D   A room where many people using IT work

23   Which one of the following is a disadvantage of office manuals?

A   Strict interpretation of instructions creates inflexibility
B   The quality of service received from suppliers is reduced
C   They create bureaucracy and demotivate staff
D   They do not facilitate the induction and training of new staff

24   Which one of the following is LEAST likely to be carried out by an Accounts Department?

A   Arrangement of payment of creditors (suppliers)
B   Calculation of wages and salaries to be paid
C   Despatch of customer orders
D   Preparation of company financial records

25   What is the main purpose of prime entry records?

A   Calculate the cash received and spent by a business
B   Prevent a large volume of unnecessary detail in the ledgers
C   Provide a monthly check on the double-entry bookkeeping
D   Separate the taxable and exempt VAT (sales tax) transactions

26   The following relate to the use of order processing software in a company:

(1)   Legislative changes may be incorporated automatically in periodic updates.
(2)   Rival companies will be able to use the same software.
(3)   The company controls development of the software.
(4)   There may be a large user group to share experiences.

Which of the above are advantages to the company of implementing a software package solution to manage order processing?

A   1 and 3 only
B   1 and 4 only
C   2 and 4 only
D   1, 3 and 4 only

27   The following relate to batch processing or to real-time processing of data:

(1)   Audit trails are easily made since the processing of data occurs at pre-determined times.
(2)   Customer queries can be responded to immediately.
(3)   Processing can be performed during the evening when the computer is not being used interactively.
(4)   The data is always up-to-date.

Which of the above are advantages of real-time processing?

A   1 and 2 only
B   1 and 3 only
C   2 and 4 only
D   1, 3 and 4 only

28   Which one of the following departments is NOT a service cost centre in a manufacturing company?

A   Accounting
B   Assembly
C   Maintenance
D   Personnel

29   A company operates a retail supermarket chain selling a range of grocery and household products. It has branches throughout the country and is reviewing the range of goods to be stocked in each of these branches.

How might the company best analyse its profitability for this purpose?

A   By area of the country
B   By contract with each supplier
C   By customer payment method
D   By product line stocked

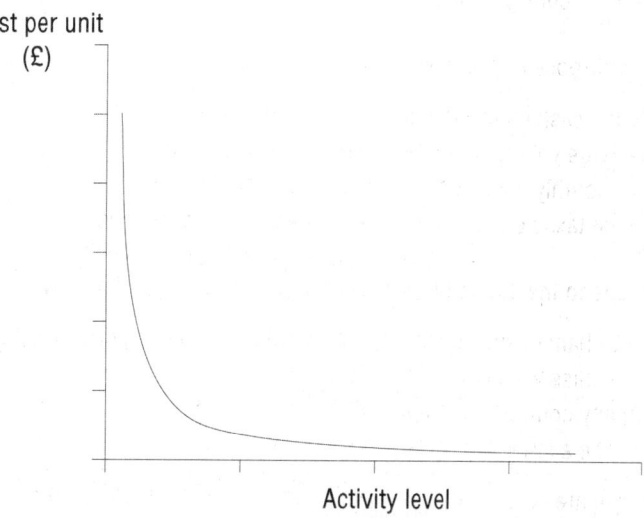

Cost per unit (£)

Activity level

30   A large hotel has coffee shops, restaurants and banqueting. They are used by hotel residents and outside users. The manager of the hotel is responsible for encouraging residents to use the hotel's catering facilities.

Which report will show how effective the manager has been in achieving this objective?

A   A report analysing the utilisation of hotel services per room occupied
B   A report showing the amount of money spent in the hotel's catering facilities
C   A report showing the number of residents in the hotel at any given time
D   A report showing the occupancy of the various catering facilities

31   Which description best fits the above cost curve?

    A   Direct labour cost per unit
    B   Direct material cost per unit
    C   Fixed production cost per unit
    D   Variable production cost per unit

32   Which one of the following items is most likely to be treated as an indirect cost by a furniture manufacturer?

    A   Fabric to cover the seat of a chair
    B   Metal used for the legs of a chair
    C   Staples to fit the fabric to the seat of a chair
    D   Wood used to make the frame of a chair

33   A company employs 20 direct production operatives and 10 indirect staff in its manufacturing department. The normal operating hours for all employees is 38 hours per week and all staff are paid a basic rate of $5 per hour. Overtime hours are paid at the basic rate + 50%. During a particular week all employees worked for 44 hours to meet the company's general production requirements.

What amount would be charged to production overhead?

    A $300
    B $450
    C $2,350
    D $2,650

34   With which costs is absorption costing concerned?

    A   Direct labour costs only
    B   Direct material costs only
    C   Fixed costs only
    D   Variable and fixed costs

35   How is total contribution calculated?

    A   Total revenue less fixed costs
    B   Total revenue less production costs
    C   Total revenue less total costs
    D   Total revenue less variable costs

36   Aspects of payroll include:

    (1)   Employer's national insurance contributions
    (2)   Employee's national insurance contributions
    (3)   Income Tax (PAYE)
    (4)   Salaries

Which of the above are costs to an employer?

    A   1 and 4 only
    B   2 and 4 only
    C   2, 3 and 4 only
    D   1, 2, 3 and 4

37   An employee is paid on a piecework basis. The scheme is as follows:

1 – 100 units per day	$0.20 per unit
101 – 200 units per day	$0.30 per unit
> 200 units per day	$0.40 per unit

Only the additional units qualify for the higher rates. Rejected units do not qualify for payment. An employee produced 210 units in a day of which 17 were rejected as faulty.

How much did the employee earn for the day?

A $47.90
B $54.00
C $57.90
D $84.00

38   It is possible for an item of overhead expenditure to be shared amongst several cost centres. It is also possible that an item of overhead expenditure may relate to just one specific cost centre.

What term is used to describe charging an item of overhead to just one specific cost centre?

A   Absorption
B   Allocation
C   Apportionment
D   Re-apportionment

39   What would be the most appropriate basis for apportioning machinery insurance costs to cost centres within a factory?

A   Floor area occupied by the machinery
B   Number of machines
C   Operating hours of machinery
D   Value of machinery

40   A firm uses a unique code to identify each customer - the first four letters of each name are followed by four digits.

Which one of the following will appear first when customers are sorted into descending order?

A   ADAM0001
B   ADAA0099
C   ADDA0100
D   ABAB0999

41   A firm maintains a stock (inventory) control database.

Which one of the following is most likely to occur when suppliers cannot deliver goods on time?

A   Customer demand will rise accordingly
B   Customer orders will not be satisfied
C   Stock levels will become too high
D   Suppliers' delivery quantities will be lowered

42   Which one of the following is the correct sequential flow of documents to complete the purchase of goods on credit?

A   Goods received note, purchase order, cheque requisition, invoice, delivery note
B   Purchase order, delivery note, goods received note, invoice, cheque requisition
C   Purchase order, goods received note, delivery note, cheque requisition, invoice
D   Purchase order, invoice, goods received note, cheque requisition, delivery note

43   Which member of staff is most likely to raise a goods received note?

    A   Delivery driver
    B   Finance director
    C   Sales ledger clerk
    D   Store clerk

44   The following statements relate to the application of feedback and feedforward control:

    (1)   Feedback and feedforward are both applied in budgetary planning and control.
    (2)   Feedback is used in the analysis of variances.
    (3)   Feedforward enables budgeted data for a period to be amended for the next period.
    (4)   Feedforward relates to the setting of performance standards.

Which of the above statements are true?

    A   1 and 2 only
    B   3 and 4 only
    C   1, 2 and 4 only
    D   1, 3 and 4 only

45   Which one of the following is the correct description of a flexible budget?

    A   A budget that can be changed according to circumstances
    B   A budget that is adjusted according to actual activity
    C   A budget that is open to negotiation
    D   A budget that is used for planning purposes only

46   A product has a budgeted direct material cost of $5 per unit. In a period, production of the product was:

Budget   9,000 units
Actual   8,800 units

$44,380 was incurred on direct materials for the period's production.

What was the direct material variance, comparing actual with the flexed budget?

    A $380 Adverse
    B $380 Favourable
    C $620 Adverse
    D $620 Favourable

47   Which one of the following is NOT a factor that should affect a decision as to whether to investigate a variance?

    A   Controllability of variance
    B   Cost of investigation
    C   Personnel involved
    D   Trend of variance

48   A company has sold 11,300 units of its single product for a total sales revenue of $88,140. Variable costs and fixed costs are $4.29 and $2.73 per unit respectively.

What is the contribution to sales ratio?

    A   10%
    B   45%
    C   55%
    D   65%

LEARNING MEDIA

49   Which one of the following is NOT an assumption used in break-even analysis?

    A   Selling price depends upon quantity sold
    B   Total variable costs increase in proportion to activity
    C   Unit fixed costs increase with a decrease in activity
    D   Unit variable costs are a constant

50   The following information is available:

Sales	$103,200	(@ $12 per unit)
Variable costs	$54,180	
Fixed costs	$38,000	

What level of sales is required to break-even?

    A   6,032 units
    B   8,600 units
    C $72,381
    D $80,000

Mock exam 1: Answers

1	B	A compiler is a special type of software tool used to help write programs. Of the four options, only a modem is hardware.
2	D	The main purpose of a mouse is not to play games!
3	D	The CPU processes instructions and data.
4	B	'Date of birth' would be a field in a database record.
5	D	
6	C	Both reasons are valid.
7	B	Modern computers don't tend to require keys to be 'unlocked'.
8	C	
9	D	A Zip disk would be a better back-up option than part of the server, as it could be stored off site.
10	A	
11	B	A fire proof locked cabinet is the best option within the office.
12	D	Personal information is covered by the Data Protection Act.
13	B	
14	D	All information should bring greater benefits than the cost of producing it – otherwise it is not worth producing.
15	C	Effective communication should be as simple as possible – complete ideas should be explained clearly.
16	D	Only this option refers to internal information.
17	A	
18	D	
19	A	The spell checker would not pick up 'bred' as it is a valid word. Grammar checkers are unreliable.
20	D	All three items are important.
21	B	
22	B	
23	A	
24	C	
25	B	
26	B	Only items 1 and 4 are valid advantages to the company of implementing the software.
27	C	Real-time systems are updated immediately, so are always up to date.
28	B	
29	D	
30	A	
31	C	The other three are variable costs and therefore would be constant amounts per unit as activity increases whereas the fixed costs remain constant in total but fall per unit as activity levels increase
32	C	Small consumables such as staples are often treated as indirect costs

33	D		$
		Indirect workers – 38 hours × $5 × 10	1,900
		6 hours × $7.50 × 10	450
		Direct workers – over time premium 6 hours × $2.50 × 20	300
			2,650

34 D

35 D

36 A The employee's national insurance contributions and PAYE (income tax) are deducted from the employees' gross pay and paid over to the Inland Revenue and are therefore not a cost to the employer

37 A Total good production 210 – 17 = 193

	$
100 @ $0.20	20.00
93 @ $0.30	27.90
	47.90

38 B

39 D The insurance cost will be based upon the value of the machinery rather than floor area occupied, number of machines or operating hours.

40 C

41 B

42 B

43 D

44 A

45 B

46 A

	$
8,800 units should have cost	44,000
But did cost	44,380
	380 Adverse

47 C

48 B

	$
Selling price $88,140/11,300	7.80
Variable cost	4.29
Contribution	3.51

Contribution to sales ratio $\dfrac{3.51}{7.80} \times 100$

$= 45\%$

49 A

50	D	Number of units sold	=	$103,200/$12
			=	8,600 units
		Variable cost per unit	=	$54,180/8,600
			=	$6.30
		Contribution per unit	=	$12.00 – 6.30
			=	$5.70
		Break even in units	=	$38,000/5.70
			=	6,666.667
		Break even in sales value	=	6,666.667 × $12 = $80,000

CAT

Introductory Paper 2
Information for Management Control

Mock Examination 2

Question Paper	
Time allowed	**2 hours**
ALL FIFTY questions are compulsory and MUST be answered	

DO NOT OPEN THIS PAPER UNTIL YOU ARE READY TO START UNDER EXAMINATION CONDITIONS

ALL FIFTY questions are compulsory and must be attempted.

Each question carries two marks

1   Which one of the following is an input device?

    A   Modem
    B   Keyboard
    C   CPU
    D   Printer

2   Which of the following storage devices has the largest capacity?

    A   Hard disk
    B   CD
    C   DVD
    D   3½" floppy disk

3   The maximum amount of data (approximately) that can be stored on a DVD is:

    A   1.44 Mb
    B   80 Mb
    C   650 Mb
    D   5 Gb

4   Which of the following statements about Local Area Networks (LANs) are correct?

    (i)   Relies on telephone lines to link it together

    (ii)   Consists of a number of independent computers which require network software to function as a network

    (iii)   Is incapable of extensive geographical dispersion

    (iv)   Is likely to contain a central server computer

    A   (i) and (iii) only
    B   (iii) and (iv) only
    C   (ii), (iii) and (iv)
    D   All four statements

5   The type of computer memory referred to as ROM may be defined as:

    A   A small capacity but extremely fast memory chip, which saves a second copy of the pieces of data most recently read from or written to main memory.

    B   A memory chip into which fixed data is written permanently at the time of manufacture. New data cannot be written into the memory

    C   Memory that is directly available to the processing unit. It holds the data and programs in current use. Data can be written onto or read from this memory

    D   An external device

6   Which one of the following is true of computer software referred to as the operating system?

    A   Is another name for application software
    B   Is not required on a stand-alone PC
    C   Provides the bridge between the user, application software and hardware
    D   Enables complex mathematical functions to be calculated

7   Which of the following options shows the different formats in which data may be entered into a spreadsheet?

A   Numbers and formulae only
B   Text and numbers only
C   Text and formulae only
D   Numbers, text and formulae

8   The Data Protection Act 1998 aims to protect:

A   Individuals from unauthorised use of data relating to them
B   Sensitive government data and information
C   Computer systems from hackers
D   Software suppliers from illegal copying

9   The process of scrambling data before transmitting it and unscrambling it upon receipt is known as:

A   Data encryption
B   Data modulation and demodulation
C   Multiplexing
D   Coding

10   The unlawful activity of attempting to gain unauthorised access to a computer system is commonly referred to as:

A   A virus
B   A Trojan
C   Hacking
D   Distorting

11   The most common cause of incorrect data in a computer system is:

A   Hacking
B   A virus
C   Hardware failure
D   Human error

12   Why should some computer back-ups be stored off site?

A   To enable working at home
B   To conform with the procedures manual
C   To ensure a backup is available should the office be damaged or destroyed
D   To save office space

13   Which one of the following statements concerning the difference between management accounts and financial accounts is incorrect?

A   Financial accounts are governed by strict accounting rules and regulations, management accounts are not

B   There is a legal requirement for management accounts

C   Management accounts are often required for individual divisions and/or products whereas financial accountants usually cover the whole company

D   Management accounts are mainly for internal purposes whereas financial accounts are mainly for external purposes

14   Which one of the following options shows three key purposes of management accounting?

    A   Planning, control and decision making
    B   Publication, control and decision making
    C   Decision making, negotiating and resourcing
    D   Planning, negotiation and resourcing

15   Which of the following is not true of good management information?

    A   Must be as accurate as required for its purpose
    B   Must be computerised
    C   Must be cost-effective
    D   Must be relevant

16   Which of the following would be data rather than information?

    A   Salesman's commission as a percentage of total sales
    B   Total sales per product as a percentage of total sales
    C   Sales increase/decrease per product in the month
    D   Total sales value per day

17   Which of the following options is not a reason for having a policy manual for an organisation?

    A   To eliminate thought and flexibility
    B   To help new employees understand policies and procedures
    C   To record health and safety procedures
    D   To set out authorisation policies

18   How would facts and figures that have been processed, analysed and communicated to another party be best described?

    A   Information
    B   Data
    C   Neither A nor B
    D   Both A and B

19   Which of the following is internal information within a purchasing function or department?

    A   Supplier's price list
    B   Purchase Invoices
    C   Requisition forms
    D   Delivery notes

20   When deciding on appropriate channel or format for communication, which factors should be considered?

    (i)   Cost
    (ii)   Speed of delivery
    (iii) Complexity
    (iv)   Number of recipients

    A   (i) and (ii)
    B   (ii) and (iv)
    C   (ii), (iii) and (iv)
    D   (i), (ii), (iii) and (iv)

21   Which of the following methods would be the most appropriate format in which to answer a formal complaint from a customer?

    A   Letter (sent either by post or as an e-mail attachment)
    B   Memo
    C   Report
    D   Presentation

22   Which of the following is not true in relation to e-mail?

    A   Information can be sent to multiple users in one message
    B   Almost instantaneous delivery
    C   Stores messages after they are received
    D   E-mail is always informal and 'off-the-record'

23   Which of the following is not normally a function of a purchasing department?

    A   Negotiating prices with suppliers
    B   Raising purchase orders
    C   Recording goods received into stock (inventory)
    D   Ensuring only authorised purchases are made

24   Which of the following staff would have the least involvement or be least affected by a transaction involving the purchase of goods on credit?

    A   Purchasing manager
    B   Sales ledger controller (receivables controller)
    C   Stores manager
    D   All of the above staff would be involved

25   What is the double entry for the sale of goods on credit?

    A   Debit Sales
               Credit Creditors (payables)

    B   Debit Creditors (payables)
               Credit Sales

    C   Debit Sales
               Credit Debtors (receivables)

    D   Debit Debtors (receivables)
               Credit Sales

26   A telephone bill has been received with a line rental of $25 per month, and a charge per call of 5c. This telephone cost could be best described as:

    A   A fixed cost
    B   A variable cost
    C   A stepped–fixed cost
    D   A mixed cost

27   Which of the following would be classified as direct expenses for a company producing tables and chairs?

(i)   The depreciation of a machine on an assembly line
(ii)   The hire cost of maintenance tools and equipment
(iii)   The cost of overtime worked by carpenters to complete a specific customer order
(iv)   The wood used in making the tables and chairs
(v)   The carpenter's wages

A   (i) and (iii)
B   (ii), (iv) and (v)
C   (iii), (iv) and (v)
D   (iv) and (v)

28   Which of the following departments is a production cost centre in a company producing milk in cartons?

A   Stores
B   Accounts
C   Packaging
D   Maintenance

29   A manager has responsibility for costs incurred, revenues earned and investment in fixed assets in one area of a business.

This manager is responsible for which one of the following?

A   A cost centre
B   A revenue centre
C   A profit centre
D   An investment centre

30   A company purchases and sells a range of bathroom accessories through a number of outlets throughout a country. Management are considering the closure of some of the retail outlets.

Which of the following is most likely to be useful for this purpose?

A   Sales by area of the country
B   Sales by outlet
C   Contribution by area of the country
D   Contribution by outlet

31   Bloomsbury Limited sell men's clothes through three different stores in London.

Bloomsbury use a seven character account coding convention – comprising the three digit store location, followed by underscore, followed by the three digit product type. An extract from Bloomsbury's coding list shows the following:

110   Sales: Holborn store
120   Sales: Kings Cross store
130   Sales: Waterloo store
001   Sales: jumpers
002   Sales: shirts
003   Sales: trousers

Which of the following is the code for sales of trousers at Holborn?

A   110_001
B   110_003
C   120_003
D   130_003

32   Which one of the following documents contains details of a payment being made?

    A   Goods received note
    B   Despatch note
    C   Sales invoice
    D   Remittance advice

33   A factory employs 25 direct production workers and 10 indirect staff. The standard working week is 40 hours. All staff are paid at the basic rate of $8 per hour with overtime paid at time and a half.

Last week all employees worked for 45 hours to meet general production requirements.

What is the direct labour charge for the week?

    A $320
    B $8,000
    C $9,000
    D $9,500

34   What would be the most appropriate basis for apportioning the insurance costs of plant and machinery to departments within a factory?

    A   Floor space (m^2) occupied by each department
    B   Number of employees in each department
    C   Number of machines in each department
    D   Value of machines in each department

35   Which of the following documents in the purchases cycle would be produced by the purchaser?

    A   Delivery note
    B   Purchase requisition
    C   Invoice
    D   Credit note

36   A sales invoice should be checked against which documents?

    A   Purchase requisition and goods received note
    B   Advice note and delivery note
    C   Goods received note and order form
    D   Sales order and despatch note

37   A manufacturing company has 20 employees, each paid a basic rate of $5 an hour. A standard working week is 35 hours; overtime is paid at time and a quarter. Last week all employees worked 37 hours, producing 3,000 units.

What is the total unit labour cost?

    A $1.23/unit
    B $1.25/unit
    C $0.06/unit
    D $1.54/unit

38   Gross pay is made up of:

    A   Cash paid to employees
    B   Cash paid to employees plus PAYE (income tax) plus employer's National Insurance contribution
    C   Cash paid to employees plus PAYE (income tax) plus employee's National Insurance contribution
    D   Cash paid to employees plus PAYE (income tax) plus employee's and employer's National Insurance contribution

39   A manufacturing company operates a piecework wage system. Each employee is paid $6.00 per unit for the first 30 units they produce each week and $7.00 per unit for units in excess of this amount. There are 50 employees.

Assuming each employee produces 37 units per week, what is the total unit labour cost?

A $6.00
B $6.05
C $6.19
D $7.00

40   Under absorption costing, allocation is most likely to be used for which of the following overheads?

A   Rent
B   Department supervisor's salary
C   Insurance
D   Electricity

41   Product Y has a budgeted direct material cost of $10 per unit. The budgeted direct material costs for the year were $110,000 (based on budgeted units of 11,000).

During the period actual production was 11,500 units and actual direct material costs were $110,000.

What was the direct material activity/volume variance, comparing the fixed budget with the flexible budget?

A   Nil
B $5,000 favourable
C $5,000 adverse
D $2,000 adverse

42   Which of the following would help to explain a favourable direct labour variance?

(i)   Employees taking less time to make each unit than expected due to additional training
(ii)   An unexpected pay rise for all employees
(iii) More units being produced than expected in the budget

A   (i) only
B   (i) and (ii)
C   (i) and (iii)
D   (i), (ii) and (iii)

43   What is exception reporting?

A   Reporting of exceptional activities within an organisation
B   Reporting of all variances to management
C   Reporting only controllable matters to management
D   Reporting of variances which exceed a certain amount only

44   Tiger Team plc's actual direct labour costs for August 20X4 were $90,200. Actual production in August 20X4 was 12,500 units compared to the 13,000 units budgeted.

The budgeted direct labour cost was $6 per week.

What is the total direct labour variance?

A $12,200 favourable
B $12,200 adverse
C $15,200 favourable
D $15,200 adverse

45   Special Saws Ltd sell one product, a specialist electric saw, for $330.

Each saw incurs variable costs of $150 and fixed costs of $90.

Budgeted sales are 2,000 units.

What is Specialist Saws Ltd's breakeven point?

    A   1,000 units
    B   1,250 units
    C   1,455 units
    D   2,000 units

46   Porter plc makes and sells puppets. For 20X4 the company has the following results:

Sales	$30/unit
Variable costs	$20/unit
Fixed costs	$165,000

Budgeted sales for 20X4 were 21,500 units

What is Porter plc's margin of safety as a percentage of budgeted sales for 20X4?

    A   11%
    B   23%
    C   30%
    D   74%

47   Which of the following statements is an appropriate definition of contribution per unit?

    A   Sales price per unit – total cost per unit
    B   Sales price per unit – fixed cost per unit
    C   Sales price per unit – variable cost per unit
    D   Sales price per unit – production cost per unit

48   A business sells a single product and the details of this product are given below:

	$
Selling price	50.00
Direct materials	15.50
Direct labour	10.25
Variable overhead	5.75
Fixed overhead	4.80
	36.30

What is the contribution to sales ratio?

    A   27%
    B   37%
    C   48.5%
    D   69%

49   What is the formula for calculating the number of units that need to be sold to reach a target profit level?

A $\dfrac{\text{Fixed costs} + \text{target profit}}{\text{Contribution per unit}}$

B $\dfrac{\text{Fixed costs}}{\text{Contribution per unit}}$

C $\dfrac{\text{Target profit}}{\text{Contribution per unit}}$

D $\dfrac{\text{Target profit}}{\text{Profit per unit}}$

50   A company makes three products. Production of these products is restricted by the amount of labour hours available.

The selling prices and costs associated with these products are shown below.

	Product		
	A	B	C
Sale price	30	25	40
Direct materials	3	4	3
Direct labour	6	6	12
Variable overhead	1	1	2
Fixed overhead	2	2	4
Costs	12	13	21
Labour hours needed	2	1	6

In what order of priority should production be undertaken to maximise profit?

A   A, B, C
B   B, C, A
C   C, A, B
D   B, A, C

Mock exam 2: Answers

1   B   The keyboard is an input device. A modem is used for communication, a printer is an output device and the CPU performs the processing function.

2   A   A DVD can hold approximately 5Gb, a CD-Rom 650mb and a floppy disk 1.44mb of data. Hard disks vary in size but a typical PC hard disk offers 5Gb – 10Gb of storage capacity.

3   D   As noted previously, a DVD can hold approximately 5Gb.

4   C   (i) is incorrect as a LAN is linked by direct cables, not by telephone lines (a WAN is linked by a telecommunications network).

5   B   A defines a cache, C defines RAM (Random Access Memory), D – ROM is generally located inside the main computer unit. Only B defines ROM (Read Only Memory).

6   C   The operating system provides a bridge between the user, application software and the hardware.

7   D   Numbers, text and formulae can all be entered into a spreadsheet.

8   A   The Data Protection Act aims to protect the privacy of individuals.

9   A   Data encryption is the process of scrambling data at the sender's end and then unscrambling it at the receiver's end, to securely transmit the data.

10   C   'Hacking' describes the process of attempting to gain unauthorised access to a computer system.

           A virus is a piece of software which infects programs and data and possibly damages them, and which replicates itself.

           Trojans hide inside a valid program and perform an unexpected act. They act like viruses, but aren't viruses as they don't replicate themselves.

11   D   Most 'computer errors' are in fact due to 'human error'.

12   C   Off-site back-ups are required to enable recovery in the event of premises being destroyed or damaged (even a fire-proof safe on-site may be damaged or destroyed).

13   B   There is a legal requirement for financial accounts but not for management accounts.

           The other three statements are all valid differences between management and financial accounts.

14   A   Management accounting helps managers plan, control and make decisions.

15   B   In some situations, good management information could be hand-written rather than computerised eg a note from a telephone conversation.

           Accuracy, cost effectiveness and relevance are all qualities required in good management information.

16   D   The other three options have been processed in the same way to provide meaningful information, whereas total sales value per day is the basic data that will require further processing.

17   A   A policy manual does not aim to eliminate thought and flexibility - it provides guidelines to be followed.

           The other three options are all reasons for having a policy manual.

18   A   Information is data that has been processed and communicated to another party.

19   C   Requisition forms are produced internally by the company detailing the purchases they want made.

           All of the other three options would be produced externally, by the supplier.

20   D   All of the factors of cost, speed of delivery, complexity of the message to be conveyed and the number of recipients of the message should be considered in determining the appropriate communication format.

21   A   A formal complaint would normally be most appropriately answered by a letter. Generally this would be posted, but if the complaint was received via e-mail the letter could be sent as an attachment via e-mail.

A memo would be used for internal purposes only.

A report would tend to be used when there is a lot of information to convey, which is unlikely in responding to a complaint.

A presentation would not be appropriate as the complaint should be dealt with between the individual and the organisation.

22   D   E-mail is increasingly being used for business dealings. As e-mail messages may be stored and printed they are definitely not 'off-the-record'.

23   C   Recording goods received into stock (inventory) would be a function of the stores department.

Options A, B, and D are useful functions of the purchasing department.

24   B   A sales ledger controller (receivables controller) deals with the recording and collection of sales made on credit.

The purchasing manager would negotiate and make the purchase and the Stores manager would be responsible for recording the goods received from the purchase.

25   D   A sale of goods on credit is recorded as:

Debit: Debtors (receivables)
Credit: Sales

26   D   The line rental is a fixed cost and the per call charge is a variable cost, making the overall bill a mixed (or semi-variable) cost.

27   C   Overtime worked specifically for customer's request is a direct cost. The wood is direct material and the carpenter's wages are direct labour.

The depreciation and hire cost can not be directly traced to units of production so are indirect costs.

28   C   All production units will have to flow through packaging to be ready for sale. They do not have to flow through any of the other departments, making these service centres.

29   D   The manager has responsibility for investment as well as costs and revenues – this is therefore an investment centre.

30   D   The company will want to consider contribution (sales revenue less variable costs) per outlet, as this is what will be lost if the outlet is closed down.

31   B

Sale by Holborn store	110
Sale of trousers	003
Correct code	110_003

32   D   A remittance advice contains details of a payment being made.

33   C

	$
Direct production workers basic pay	
25 workers × 40 hours × $8 per hour	8,000
Direct production workers overtime	
25 workers × 5 hours × $8 per hour	1,000
Direct labour charge	9,000

The overtime premium cost is an indirect cost. The indirect workers basic pay is also an indirect cost

34   D   Number of machines could be used, but as the insurance premiums payable are driven by the value of the items being insured, the value of the machines is the most appropriate basis.

| 35 | B | Only the purchase requisition form is produced by the purchaser. The delivery note, invoice and credit note would all be generated by the supplier. |

36 D The sales invoice should be checked to the sales order to confirm only prices agreed on the order are being used, and to the despatch note to ensure the items being invoiced are the items that have been despatched to the customer.

37 B

Basic pay	$
20 employees × $5 per hour × 35 hours	3,500
Overtime	
20 employees × $5 per hour × 1.25 × 2 hours	250
Total labour cost	3,750
Total units	3,000
Labour cost per unit	1.25

38 C Employer's National Insurance contributions are part of total labour cost, but not part of gross pay.

39 C

1st 30 units	$
30 units × $6 per unit	180
Next 7 units	
7 units × $7 per unit	49
Total labour cost	229
Total units	37
Labour cost per unit (229/37)	6.19

40 B Overheads are allocated where they relate to only one department/cost centre. This is most likely to be the case for a department supervisor's salary.

41 C

Budgeted production volume	11,000	units
Actual production volume	11,500	units
Activity variance in units	500	units (adverse)
× budgeted cost per unit	× $10	
Activity variance	$5,000	(adverse)

42 A Statement (i) is correct, improved efficiency will result in a favourable direct labour variance.

Statement (ii) is incorrect as an unexpected pay rise will result in actual costs being higher than the budgeted costs and an adverse variance.

Statement (iii) is incorrect as the variance is the difference between the flexed budget (which is the actual production × budgeted direct labour cost per unit) and the actual results.

43 D Exception reporting involves reporting variances in excess of a certain amount or percentage of the budgeted figure.

44 B

	$
Should have cost 13,000 units × $6 per unit	78,000
Actual labour cost	90,200
Direct labour variance	12,200 (adverse)

45 A $\quad$ BEP $= \dfrac{\text{Total fixed costs}}{\text{Contribution per unit}}$

$\quad = \dfrac{\text{Total fixed costs}}{\text{Sales price per unit - variable cost per unit}}$

$\quad = \dfrac{2{,}000 \times \$90}{\$330 - \$150}$

$\quad = \dfrac{180{,}000}{\text{£}180}$

$\quad = 1{,}000$ units

46 B $\quad$ BEP $= \dfrac{\text{Total fixed costs}}{\text{Contribution per unit}}$

$\quad = \dfrac{\text{Total fixed costs}}{\text{Sales price per unit - variable cost per unit}}$

$\quad = \dfrac{165{,}000}{30 - 20}$

$\quad = 16{,}500$ units

Margin of safety $= \dfrac{\text{Budgeted sales - BEP}}{\text{Budgeted sales}} \times 100\%$

$\quad = \dfrac{21{,}500 - 16{,}500}{21{,}500} \times 100\%$

$\quad = 23\%$

47 C $\quad$ Contribution per unit = sales price per unit – variable cost per unit

48 B

	$	$
Selling price		50
Less: variable costs		
Direct materials	15.50	
Direct labour	10.25	
Variable overhead	5.75	
		(31.50)
Contribution per unit		18.50

Contribution to sales ratio $= \dfrac{\text{Contribution per unit}}{\text{Selling price per unit}} \times 100\%$

$\quad = \dfrac{18.50}{50} \times 100\%$

$\quad = 37\%$

49 A $\quad$ The correct formula is: $\dfrac{\text{Fixed costs + target profit}}{\text{Contribution per unit}}$

50   D

	Product		
	A	B	C
Selling price	30	25	40
Less: variable costs			
Direct materials	(3)	(4)	(3)
Direct labour	(6)	(6)	(12)
Variable overhead	(1)	(1)	(2)
Contribution per unit	20	14	23
Labour hours per unit	2	1	6
Contribution per labour hour	10	14	3.83
Ranking	②	①	③

REVIEW FORM & FREE PRIZE DRAW

All original review forms from the entire BPP range, completed with genuine comments, will be entered into one of two draws on 31 July 2007 and 31 January 2008. The names on the first four forms picked out on each occasion will be sent a cheque for £50.

Name: _____   Address: _____

_____

Date:_____   _____

How have you used this Practice & Revision Kit?
(Tick one box only)

☐ Home study (book only)

☐ On a course: college _____

☐ With 'correspondence' package

☐ Other _____

Why did you decide to purchase this Practice & Revision Kit? *(Tick one box only)*

☐ Have used complementary Interactive Text

☐ Have used BPP Texts in the past

☐ Recommendation by friend/colleague

☐ Recommendation by a lecturer at college

☐ Saw advertising in journals

☐ Saw website

☐ Other _____

During the past six months do you recall seeing/receiving any of the following?
(Tick as many boxes as are relevant)

☐ Our advertisement in *ACCA Student Accountant*

☐ Other advertisement _____

☐ Our brochure with a letter through the post

Which (if any) aspects of our advertising do you find useful?
(Tick as many boxes as are relevant)

☐ Prices and publication dates of new editions

☐ Information on Practice & Revision Kit content

☐ Facility to order books off-the-page

☐ None of the above

Have you used the companion Interactive Text for this subject?   ☐ Yes   ☐ No

Your ratings, comments and suggestions would be appreciated on the following areas

	Very useful	Useful	Not useful
Introductory section (How to use this Practice & Revision Kit)	☐	☐	☐
'Do You Know' checklists	☐	☐	☐
'Did You Know' checklists	☐	☐	☐
Possible pitfalls	☐	☐	☐
Objective test questions	☐	☐	☐
Short-form questions	☐	☐	☐
Content of answers	☐	☐	☐
Mock exams	☐	☐	☐
Structure & presentation	☐	☐	☐
Icons	☐	☐	☐

	Excellent	Good	Adequate	Poor
Overall opinion of this Kit	☐	☐	☐	☐

Do you intend to continue using BPP Interactive Texts/Kits?   ☐ Yes   ☐ No

Please note any further comments and suggestions/errors on the reverse of this page.

Please return to: Mary Maclean, BPP Learning Media Ltd, FREEPOST, London, W12 8BR

REVIEW FORM & FREE PRIZE DRAW (continued)

Please note any further comments and suggestions/errors below